RUSS SHIPTON'S
Rock & Pop Guitar
CHORDBOOK

CONTENTS

First published 1986
© International Music Publications

Exclusive Distributors
International Music Publications
Southend Road, Woodford Green,
Essex IG8 8HN, England

215-2-396

MUSIC CATEGORIES FOR CHORDS

(1) SIMPLE POP / FOLK ROCK / PUNK / COUNTRY

(2) BLUES ROCK / BOOGIE / HEAVY METAL

(3) GENERAL POP / REGGAE / DISCO

(4) JAZZ ROCK / LATIN / FUNK

Music Categories

In order to make the use of chords and song arranging much easier and more useful for guitar students, the chords in the "Rock & Pop Guitar Chordbook" have been split into 4 music areas:

(1) Simple Pop / Folk Rock / Punk / Country

For the beginner, the first section is the one to explore. These trypes of music generally use chord shapes at the end of the fretboard – often involving open strings.

(2) Blues Rock / Boogie / Heavy Metal

The three types of music here have one thing in common – the blues influence. This means they often involve "blue" notes in the melody, accompaniment chords and lead riffs.

(3) General Pop / Reggae / Disco

Most pop guitarists use full shapes in the middle and upper areas of the fretboard. The positions and fingerings shown for the chords in this category are perhaps the most versatile and widely used by guitarists. In the notes before the chord pages in this section I explain how shortened versions of these full chord shapes are used, particularly in disco guitar accompaniments.

(4) Jazz Rock / Latin / Funk

To produce a jazzy feel in music, chord "extensions" must be used. In other words the chords include more than the three basic notes of the usual major and minor chords. Major 7th and minor 7th chords are particularly important in all three types of music within this category.

Crossover

There are very hazy lines between the chord positions given for the different categories, so feel free to borrow shapes from one area of music to use in another. The chords given in each category are not *exclusive* to that category, they are just those *more likely* to be used for the particular music involved.

Experiment by using different chord shapes, fingerings and positions in your accompaniments and see what variety of effects and sequences you can produce.

CHORDS IN MAJOR KEYS

I	II	III	IV	V	VI	VII
(A)	Bm	C♯m	(D)	(E)	F♯m	G♯m♭5
(C)	Dm	Em	(F)	(G)	Am	Bm♭5
(D)	Em	F♯m	(G)	(A)	Bm	C♯m♭5
(E)	F♯m	G♯m	(A)	(B)	C♯m	D♯m♭5
(G)	Am	Bm	(C)	(D)	Em	F♯m♭5

Chords By Key

The 5 major keys most used by guitarists are A, C, D, E, & G. The chords that are made up from the notes in these keys are shown above – these are the chords to be "expected" in accompaniments for melodies written in these keys.

3 Main Chords

The three main chords that will normally be used in an accompaniment are those shown circled above. They are the I, IV & V chords of a key (i.e. built on the 1st, 4th & 5th notes of the major scale). Hundreds of simple songs can be accompanied on the guitar with just these three chords. In the key of A Major, for example, the three main chords are A, D & E.

The three main chords in each key are so important that I've concentrated on the various shapes and possibilities of just these chords in the layout of the book. The minor chords are dealt with together, at the end of each section. The layout of the chord pages is discussed overleaf.

Major & Minor Chords

The major chords are the most common and "ordinary" sounding chords, and as mentioned above, the three major chords of those to be expected in an accompaniment are almost bound to be used. The II, III & VI chords are minor chords – they have a slightly melancholy sound about them. One or more of them may be used with the major chords in an accompaniment. The VII chord in a key i.e. the one built on the 7th note of the major scale, is more unusual and not often used (exept in jazzy arrangements – see page 79).

Extended Chords

You'll see chords in the "Rock & Pop Guitar Chordbook" with a 7 or 9 next to the chord letter name. These chords are called "extended chords" because another note or more has been added to them.

The most common extended chords are major 7th and minor 7th chords (maj7 & m7). When the standard major & minor chords have an extra note added to them – another "3rd" in music parlance – they become 7th chords.

When the I & IV major chords include a 7th note they normally become maj7 chords. When the minor chords add a 7th note they become m7 chords. When the Vth chord adds a 7th note it becomes a "dominant" 7th (7). Here are the chords of the five keys above when they are extended to become 7th chords:

Amaj7	Bm7	C♯m7	Dmaj7	E7	F♯m7	G♯m7♭5
Cmaj7	Dm7	Em7	Fmaj7	G7	Am7	Bm7♭5
Dmaj7	Em7	F♯m7	Gmaj7	A7	Bm7	C♯m7♭5
Emaj7	F♯m7	G♯m7	Amaj7	B7	C♯m7	D♯m7♭5
Gmaj7	Am7	Bm7	Cmaj7	D7	Em7	F♯m7♭5

Chord Composition

The individual notes in chords are shown and discussed on pages 8, 26, 62 & 80.

3

THE LAYOUT OF CHORDS

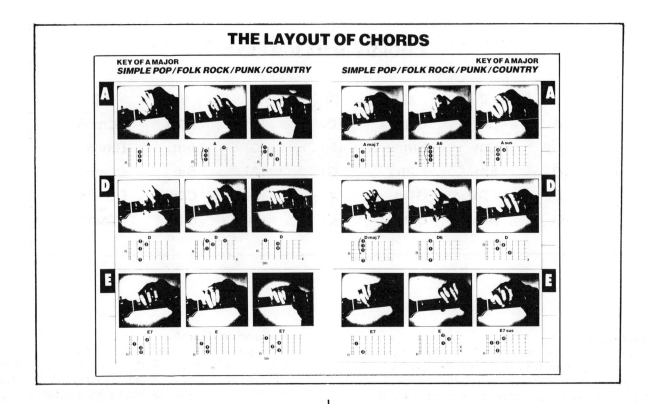

Chord Layout

An example of the double page layout for the major chords in a particular key is shown above. 6 different shapes or fingerings are given for the I chord of the key – A in the key of A Major. Each chord position is shown on a diagram as well as in a photo to make the fingering absolutely clear.

Beneath the 6 possibilities for the I chord of the key are 6 alternatives for the IV chord of the key – D in the key of A Major. At the bottom of the double page spread are 6 shapes that can be used for the V chord of the key – E in the key of A Major.

Substitute Chords

Instead of the usual chord, an extended chord may sometimes be given as an alternative – usually a 7th chord. As shown on the previous page, the maj 7th chord may be used as a substitute for the I & IV chords in a major key and a dominant 7th (written just "7") for the V chord of the key.

Group Of 3 Chords

As mentioned on the previous page, you'll normally use at least the 3 main chords to accompany a song in a major key – the I, IV & V chords, i.e. A, D & E chords in the key of A Major. Therefore it follows that you could try one of the 6 shapes given for the I chord, one for the IV chord and one for the V chord.

Guitarists generally use "compatible" shapes for the different chords in an accompaniment, which means shapes from the same area of the fretboard and possibly shapes involving the same strings of the guitar being sounded.

I have arranged the chords into groups of 3 "compatible" shapes so you can use any group of chords in a vertical line together. As with the chord music categories, these groups of three chord shapes aren't mutually exclusive. Experiment with the different chord shapes given by switching them around as well.

Minor Chords

Minor Chords that occur in the 5 most used major keys – A, C, D, E & G – are given on double pages in alphabetical order for each section. There are 3 alternatives for each chord. G♯m is the III chord in the key of E, but is not shown. Use the same shapes given for F♯m and move up two frets.

Minor Keys

As well as being used in song accompaniments written in major keys, minor chords also occur, of course, in minor keys. Each minor key is RELATIVE to THE MAJOR KEY which begins on the note 3 SEMITONES (frets) HIGHER i.e. the key of A Minor is relative to C Major. The expected chords to accompany a song in a minor key are basically the same as those used in the relative major i.e. in A Minor:

I	II	III	IV	V	VI	VII
Am	Bm♭5	C	Dm	Em	F	G
				(E)		

The minor chord in the V position of a minor key is often played as a major.

The 3 simple minor keys most used are Am, Dm & Em. Em is the relative of G, but the relative of Dm is F. Here are the expected chords in Dm:

Dm, Em♭5, F, Gm, Am (A), B♭ & C

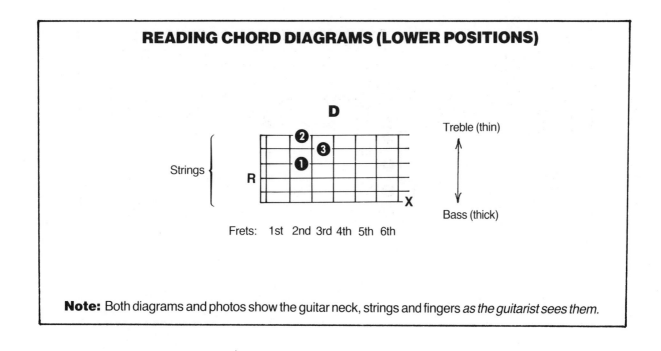

Note: Both diagrams and photos show the guitar neck, strings and fingers *as the guitarist sees them.*

Lower Position Chord Shapes

The diagrams for chords fingered within the first six frets are shown as above. The end of guitar fretboard (the "nut") is shown as a double line, and the fretwires go across the strings vertically. If you're not familiar with chord diagrams, read the following notes carefully and you'll have no problem decyphering them:

(1) Chord Name – the chord name is given above each diagram. Letters on their own (like D above) mean a normal major chord.

(2) Strings – the lowest string in both pitch and position on the diagrams is the 6th and thickest string. This produces an E note when played "open" i.e. with no finger on it. The strings go from bass to treble with the top or 1st string being highest in pitch. The open 1st string is also an E note – 2 octaves higher than the open 6th string.

(3) Frets – as mentioned above, the vertical lines going across the strings represent the fretwires in the guitar fretboard. The space between two fretwires is a fret, except the 1st fret which lies between the nut at the end of the guitar neck and the first fretwire. 6 frets are shown on every diagram in the "Rock & Pop Guitar Chordbook".

(4) Finger Numbers – the numbers in circles on the strings represent the fingers to be used to press down at the fret shown. 1 = the index finger, 2 = the middle finger, 3 = the ring finger, and 4 = the little finger. Fingertips should be used to press down, *just behind the fretwire in front.* The further away from the fretwire, the harder you'll have to press down to produce a clear note.

Thus for the D Chord above, you need to place your 1st finger on the 3rd string at the 2nd fret, your 2nd or middle finger on the 1st string at the 2nd fret, and your 3rd or ring finger on the 2nd string at the 3rd fret. Here is a photo of the D chord in the diagram above:

(5) String Not Played – when an "x" is placed next to a string, that string shouldn't be sounded. Generally this is because the note isn't part of the chord. The 6th string in the D chord above should not be played.

(6) Open Strings – an open string is an unfretted one i.e. has no finger pressing down on it. Those strings with no finger number on them can be played open – provided there is no "x" next to them. Thus the open 4th and 5th strings can be played open in the D chord shown above.

(7) The Root Note – the root note of the chord is the most important note of the chord. It's the note with the same name as the chord. This is the note which the chord is "built on". The "R" indicates the lowest root note in the chord shape (there may be more than one root note). Thus the R is placed next to the open 4th string in the D chord above, because this is the lowest D note. Another D note is the 3rd fret note on the 2nd string. Knowing where the root notes are will help you to remember and work out chord shapes.

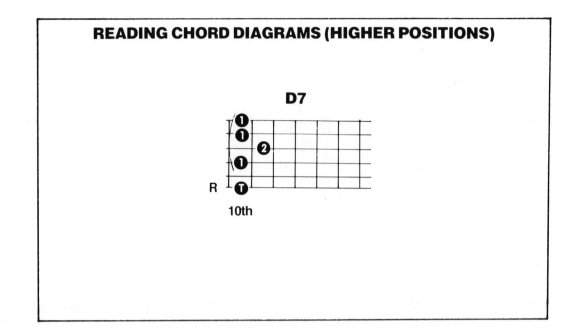

READING CHORD DIAGRAMS (HIGHER POSITIONS)

D7

R

10th

Higher Position Chords
When the chord shape is fingered higher up the
fretboard than the 6th fret, the strings are shown open-
ended as above. The lowest fret of the shape is
indicated beneath the diagram. Thus the D7 chord
above is fingered on the 10th & 11th frets.

Using The Left Hand Thumb
It's quite common for guitarists to use the left hand
thumb to fret notes on the 6th string, though it's usually
optional as you'll see when you examine the different
fingering possibilities given in this book. The large "T"
on the 6th string above indicates that the left hand
thumb comes round from the back of the neck to fret the
6th string at the 10th fret.

The Bar
Sometimes a left hand finger must press down more
than one string at the same time – this involves
something called a bar or barré. The 1st finger is used
to bar across the top 4 strings in the D7 chord above,
though the pressure need only be firm on the 1st, 2nd &
4th strings – the 2nd finger is on the 3rd string.

Open Strings
If strings have no finger indication on them and no "x"
next to them, they can be played open – even when the
shape is higher up the fretboard. Thus the 5th string can
be played open in the D7 chord above.

To make sure you're fingering the above shape
correctly, here is a photo of the chord:

CHORD GROUP ①

SIMPLE POP / FOLK ROCK / PUNK / COUNTRY

SIMPLE POP / FOLK ROCK / PUNK / COUNTRY

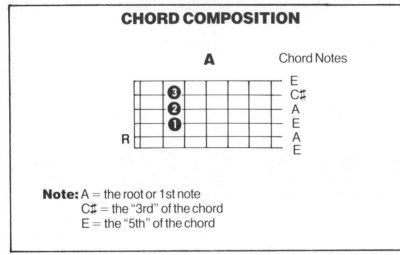

CHORD COMPOSITION

A   Chord Notes

E
C♯
A
E
A
E

Note: A = the root or 1st note
C♯ = the "3rd" of the chord
E = the "5th" of the chord

Chord Notes

Simple major & minor chords are composed of just three notes, but the shapes played by guitarists normally involve doubling up (or tripling) notes with the same letter name with the use of octaves – then the resulting chord shape produces a much fuller sound. The A major chord above (A for short), for example, consists of A, C♯ & E notes, but there are two A notes and three E's.

The Minor Chord

The minor chord with the same root note as the major has the same 5th note as well i.e. Am has A & E notes just like A (major). The difference between major and minor is the "3rd" note which is one semitone lower in the minor chord i.e. Am has a C natural note whereas A (major) has a C♯.

Most straightforward song accompaniments in the areas of music in this category will involve the common major and minor 3-note chords.

Inversions

You may hear guitarists with some theoretical knowledge talking about inversions. In strict terms, a chord inversion occurs when the lowest note sounded is *not the root note* of the chord. In a general sense, every different order of notes for a chord can be called an inversion.

If the low E note is sounded for the A chord shown above, the chord is then in strict terms an inversion. Often guitarist will play from the root note – in this case missing the 6th string.

Extended Chords

Occasionally songs of the music types in this section use extended chords – "extended" because another note is added to the 3 notes of the basic chord. Sometimes the major 7th or major 6th chord is used instead of the common major chords for the I or IV chords of the major key. In the key of A Major, for example, an Amaj7 or A6 can be substituted for the A chord, and a Dmaj7 or D6 for the D.

The V chord in a key – the E in the key of A Major – becomes a dominant 7th chord when extended. The E7 chord will often be used instead of the E chord in the key of A Major, for example.

Here are the notes of an Amaj7 chord:

A maj 7

E
C♯
G♯
E
A
E

The Amaj7 has 4 notes: A, C♯, E & G♯. In this particular shape, there are three E's and only one A – as with the common A chord, the low E note may not always be played.

With the help of the information on the next page, work out the notes of the other chords in this section.

Sus Chords

The sus chord (sustained 4th or sus4) is given as an alternative to the I & V chords in a key. The sus chord is widely used in many types of rock and pop music and usually "resolves" to i.e. changes to the same chord without the sus note. You'll notice that the fingering of the sus chord often includes the standard chord fingering as well.

Thus A sus can be used instead of the A chord, and the E7sus can be used instead of the E or E7 chord in the key of A Major. The function of the sus chord is to create a sense of movement and/or more interest in the accompaniment when the same chord would otherwise be used for several bars.

SIMPLE POP/FOLK ROCK/PUNK/COUNTRY

USING THE CAPO

Transposing With The Capo

Particular effects can be produced on the guitar only in certain keys – that's because of the different shapes that are involved. If the accompaniment is fine except for the pitch not matching the singer's vocal range, the song can be transposed to another key using the capo.

In the photo above, a capo is placed on the 3rd fret and a G chord fingered. Thus the capo has shortened the fretboard by 3 frets – and the pitch of all the strings is raised by 3 frets (three semitones in musical terms). The G chord that is being fingered is actually a B♭. The capo allows the guitarist to use familiar and easy chord shapes while playing in unusual keys like B♭.

Follow the information about notes on the fretboard, given later on this page, and you'll be able to work out what key you're playing in while using the capo.

Transposing With Moveable Shapes

Most rock & pop electric guitarists don't use the capo – instead they finger moveable shapes and move them up and down the fretboard to transpose accompaniments. These "moveable shapes" are explained in later sections of the book.

Finding Notes On The Guitar

In order to transpose efficiently and quickly, to find chord shapes and arrange accompaniments effectively, it's advisable to learn the notes on the guitar fretboard. You need to know three things:

(1) Open String Notes

Notes

(2) 1 Semibreve = 1 Fret – you need to know that the smallest step in pitch for Western music is a semitone – this is equal to one fret on the guitar.

(3) ♯ & ♭ Notes – lastly you need to remember that between all the notes EXCEPT B & C and E & F, there is an intermediary note. These notes are called ♯ or ♭ (sharp or flat) depending on the context. Here are the 1st or top string notes as an example:

1st String Notes

Fret →

1	2	3	4	5	6	7	8	9	10	11	12	13	14
E	F	F♯	G	G♯	A	A♯	B	C	C♯	D	D♯	E	F	F♯

E F F♯ G G♯ A A♯ B C C♯ D D♯ E F F♯
   (G♭)   (A♭)   (B♭)   (D♭) (E♭)   (G♭)

Draw a diagram of the guitar fretboard up to the 5th fret and fill in all the notes. Try to relate some of them to the chords you've learnt.

KEY OF A MAJOR
SIMPLE POP / FOLK ROCK / PUNK / COUNTRY

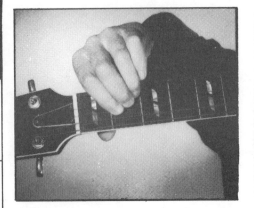

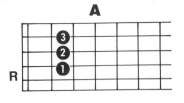

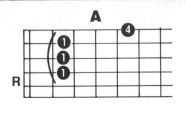

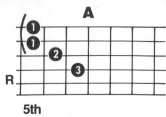

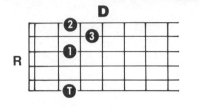

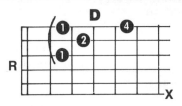

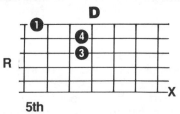

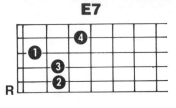

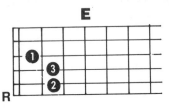

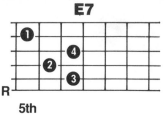

SIMPLE POP / FOLK ROCK / PUNK / COUNTRY

A

A maj 7

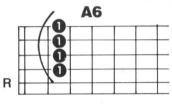
A6

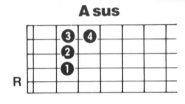
A sus

D

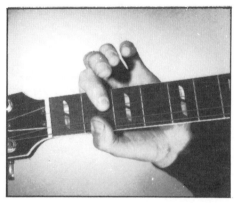

D maj 7

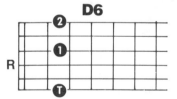
D6

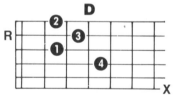
D

E

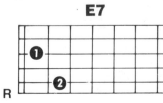
E7

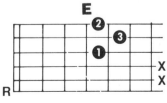
E

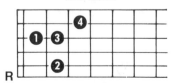
E7 sus

KEY OF C MAJOR
SIMPLE POP / FOLK ROCK / PUNK / COUNTRY

C

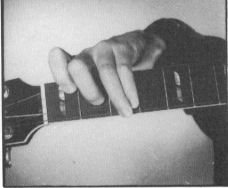

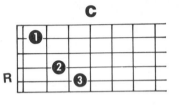
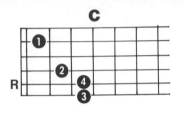
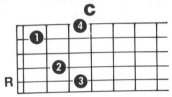

C   C   C

F

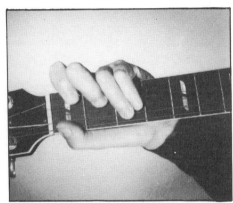

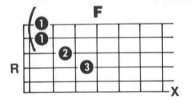
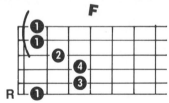
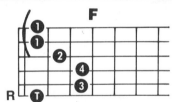

F   F   F

G

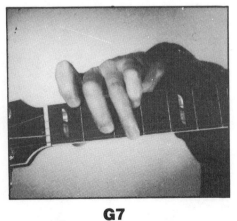

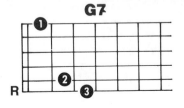
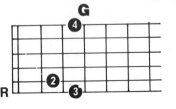

G7   G   G7

SIMPLE POP / FOLK ROCK / PUNK / COUNTRY

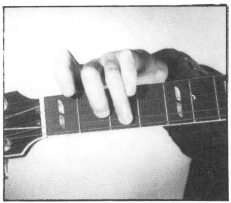
C maj 7

C6
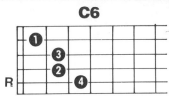

C sus
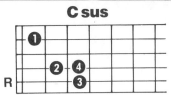

F maj 7

F6
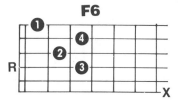

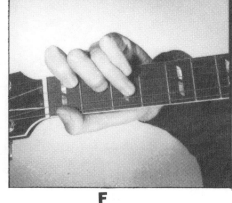
F
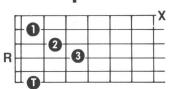

G
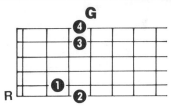

G7
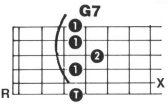

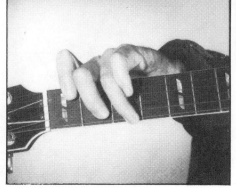
G7 sus
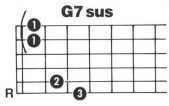

C
F
G

13

D

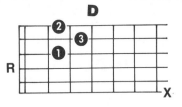

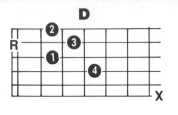

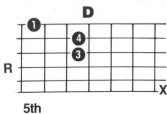

G

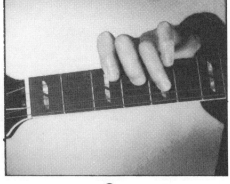

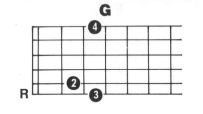

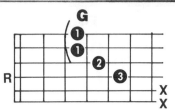

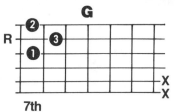

A

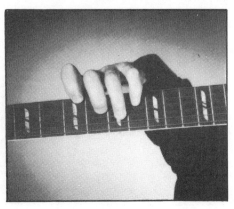

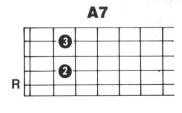

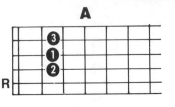

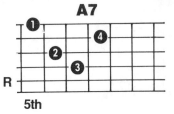

SIMPLE POP / FOLK ROCK / PUNK / COUNTRY

D

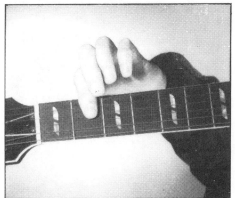

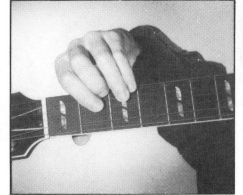

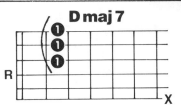
D maj 7

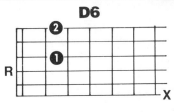
D6

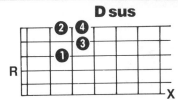
D sus

G

G maj 7

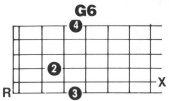
G6

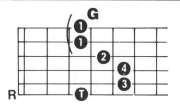
G

A

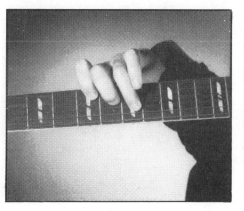

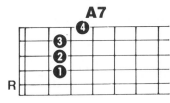
A7

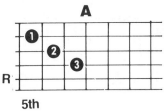
A

5th

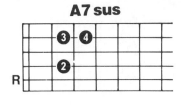
A7 sus

E

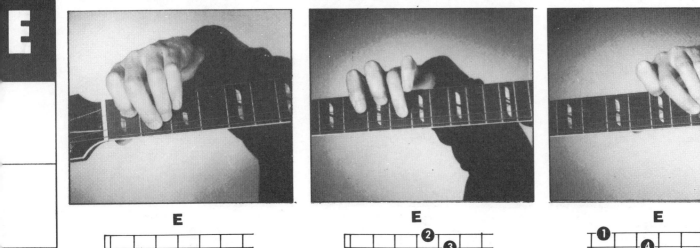

E

E

E

7th

A

A

A

A

B

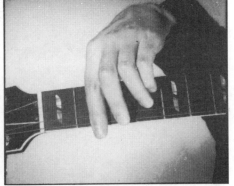
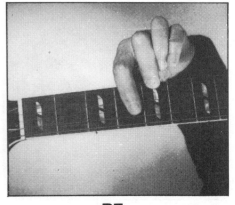

B7

B7

B7

E

E maj 7

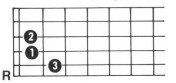

E6

E sus

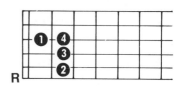

A

A maj 7

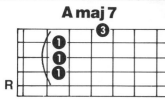

A6

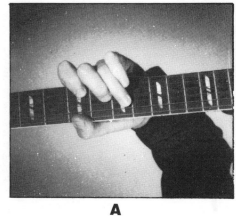

A

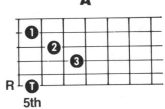

5th

B

B7

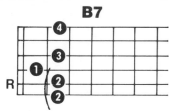

B

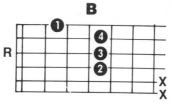

B7 sus

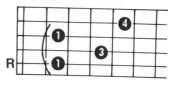

G

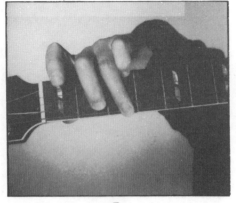

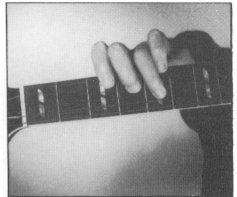

G

G

G

C

C

C (G bass)

C

D

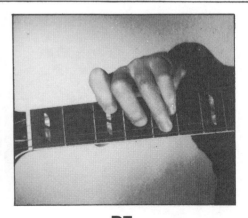

D7

D

D7

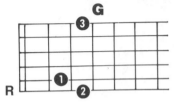
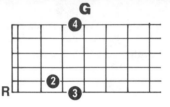
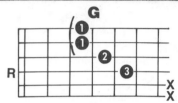
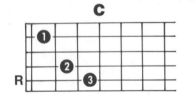
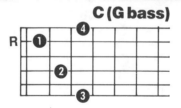
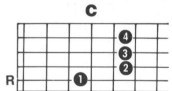
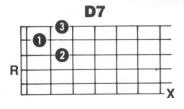
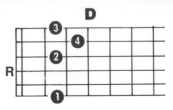
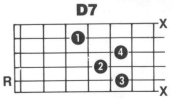

SIMPLE POP / FOLK ROCK / PUNK / COUNTRY

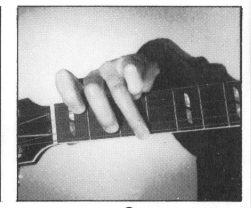

G

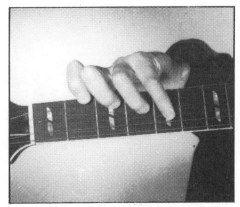

G maj 7

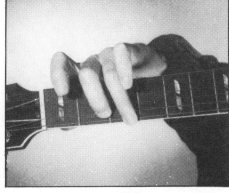

G6

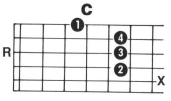

G sus

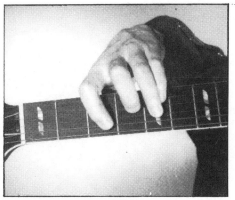

C

C maj 7

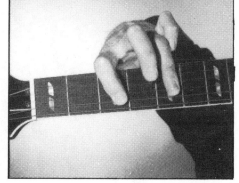

C6

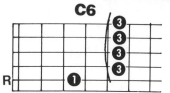

C

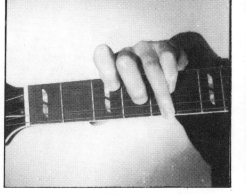

D

D9

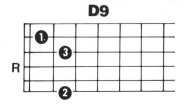

D9

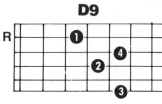

D7 sus

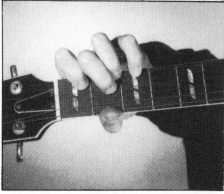

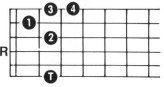

MINOR CHORDS
SIMPLE POP / FOLK ROCK / PUNK / COUNTRY

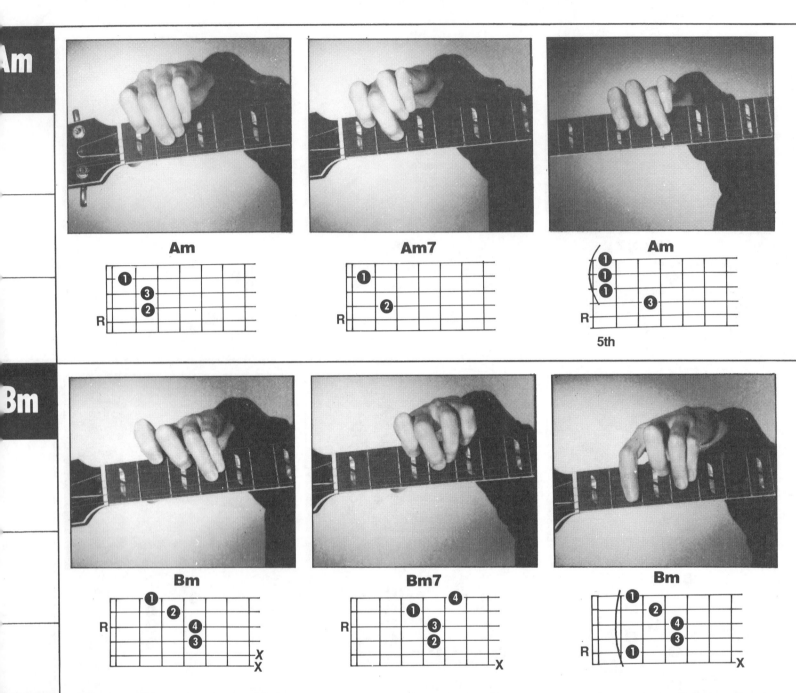

Am   Am

Am7

Am   5th

Bm

Bm

Bm7

Bm

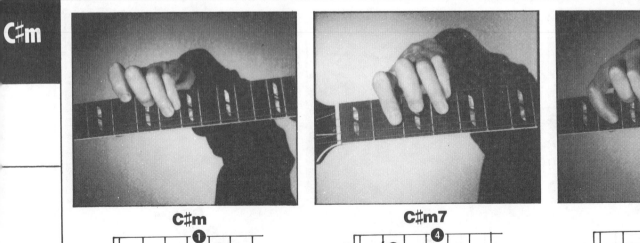

C#m

C#m

C#m7

C#m

Dm

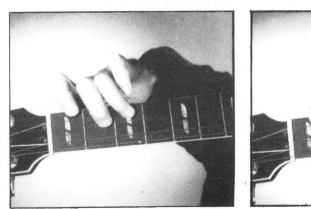

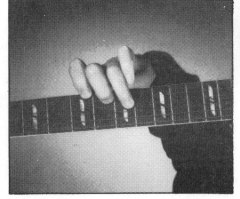

Dm

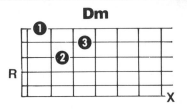

Dm7

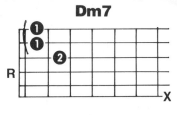

Dm

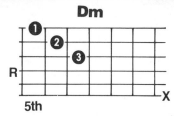

5th

Em

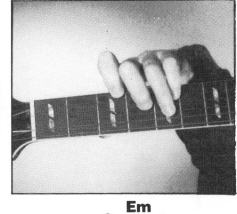

Em

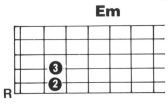

Em7

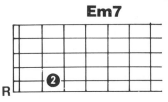

Em

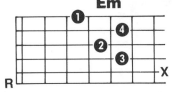

F#m

F#m

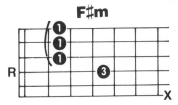

F#m7

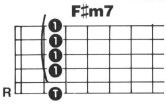

F#m

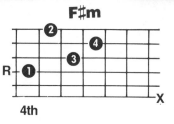

4th

SIMPLE POP / FOLK ROCK / PUNK / COUNTRY
SAMPLE CHORD SEQUENCE — COUNTRY ¾ SWING Band 2, Side 1 on record

Notes: Beat marks are given beneath the tablature which is divided into bars. The numbers on the strings are FRET NUMBERS and the arrows mean strums (↑ = downstrum). Use the chord shapes shown above each chord name.

Tablature is explained fully in the introductory book to "Rock & Pop Guitar". The rhythm pattern below and right hand technique is explained in Book 1.

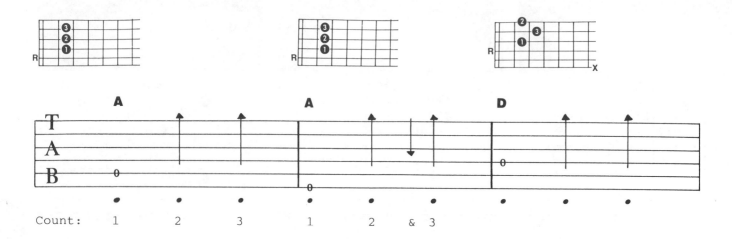

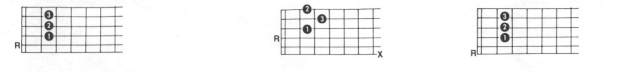

Count: 1   2   3   1   2   &   3

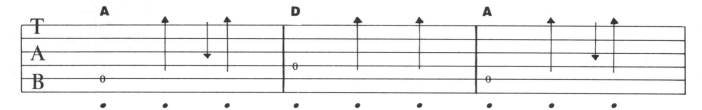

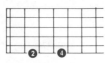

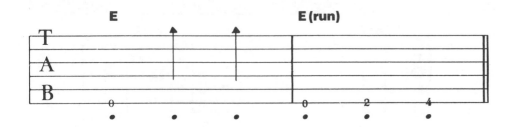

SIMPLE POP/FOLK ROCK/PUNK/COUNTRY

SAMPLE CHORD SEQUENCE — FOLK ROCK ⁴/₄   Band 3, Side 1 on record

Notes: Beat marks are given beneath the tablature which is divided into bars. The arrows on the strings are strums (↑ = downstrum). Use the chord shapes shown above each chord name.

Tablature is explained fully in the introductory book to "Rock & Pop Guitar". The rhythm pattern below and right hand technique required are explained in Book 2.

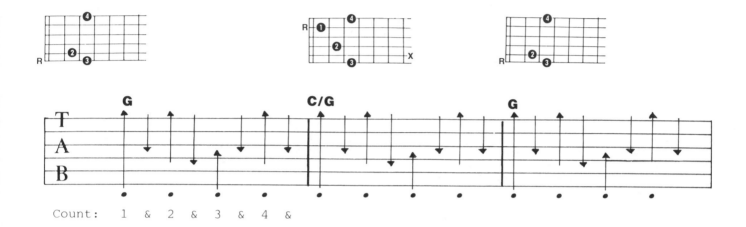

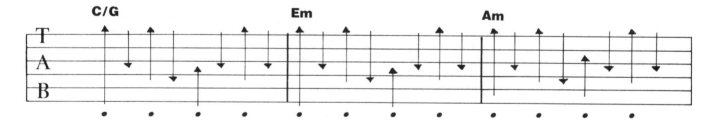

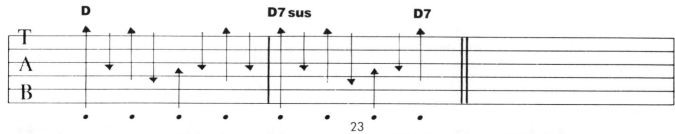

SIMPLE POP/FOLK ROCK/PUNK/COUNTRY

SAMPLE CHORD SEQUENCE – SIMPLE POP 6/8 Band 4, Side 1 on record

Notes: Beat marks are given beneath the tablature which is divided into bars. The numbers on the strings are FRET NUMBERS. Use the chord shapes shown above each chord name.

Tablature is explained fully in the introductory book to "Rock & Pop Guitar". The rhythm pattern below and right hand technique is explained in Book 1.

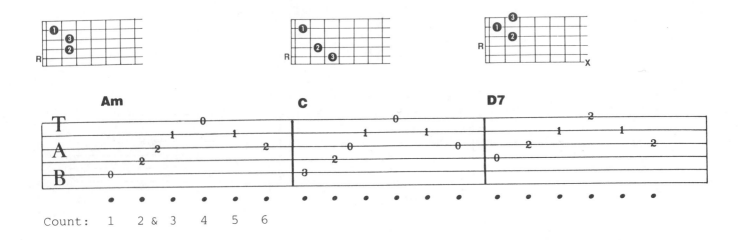

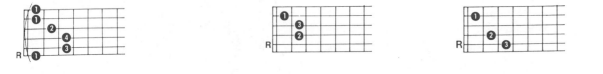

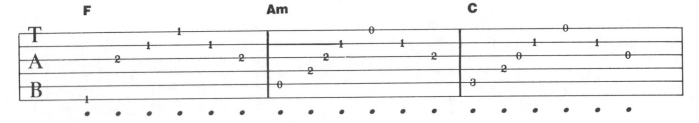

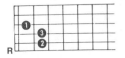

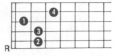

CHORD GROUP ②

BLUES ROCK / BOOGIE / HEAVY METAL

BLUES ROCK / BOOGIE / HEAVY METAL

CHORD COMPOSITION

A7

```
R
                    G
                    C#
                    A
                    E
                    A
                    E
```

Note: G = the ♭7 of the A7 chord

"Blue" Notes

The Rock 'N Roll music of the 1950's included a mixture of country and blues music. Blues music came from black American musicians and they had incorporated "blue" or flattened notes from African singing. These blue notes can be found today in rock, boogie and heavy metal styles – in melodies, lead riffs and chord accompaniments.

Dominant 7th Used As I Chord

The most common of the flattened notes in blues influenced music is the flattened 7th note. When the I & IV chords of a key are extended, the additional note comes from the major scale of the key – and the chords become maj7 chords. Only the V chord of the key becomes a dominant 7th (7 for short) chord. In bluesy accompaniments the added 7th note is flattened by a semitone (or fret) and the I & IV chords of the key are played as dominant 7th chords. Thus in the key of A Major, for example, blues accompaniments often involve the A7 and D7 chords as well as the E7. The A7 chord notes are given above – the G natural note is the flattened 7th note (flattened by one semitone or fret from G♯).

♭3 and ♭5 Notes

The ♭7 "blue" note is often added to chordal accompaniments for bluesy songs. Two other "blue" notes, also flattened by a semitone or fret from the "expected" pitch, the ♭3 and ♭5 are occasionally included in chords, but more usually come into lead guitar (or other instrument) riffs. In the key of A, these ♭3 and ♭5 notes are C natural and E♭.

The Blues Sequence

Most of the old blues songs which had such a strong influence on rock music involved a repeating chord sequence, often 12 bars in length. This is a typical sequence that made up a blues song accompaniment (each letter represents one bar or 4 beats):

E	E	E	E7
A	A7	E	E7
B7	A7	E	B7

The Triplet Rhythm

Blues music was almost always "swung".
The underlying rhythmic feel was a triplet of notes per beat:

Often the middle note was omitted to produce a swing rhythm (or shuffle if the tempo was faster). Rock 'N Roll sometimes dispensed with the swing feel, and now rock music with blues influence rarely uses triplets or a swing – blues rock is played with a hard, straight and driving rhythm these days.

BLUES ROCK/BOOGIE/HEAVY METAL

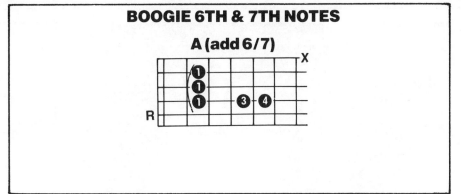

BOOGIE 6TH & 7TH NOTES

A (add 6/7)

The Boogie Effect

I've used the word "boogie" to cover the blues influenced arrangements that add 6th or 6th and 7th notes in a regular and rhythmic way. Sometimes boogie songs have a swing or shuffle feel, more often they don't. In Book 2 of the "Rock & Pop Guitar" course several accompaniments are given in full and analysed. Many other titles are listed under swing and straight rhythm headings.

In the chord shapes given in this section of the book you'll notice some diagrams shown like the one above. In a sense this diagram gives you three chords in one – the A chord is just the bar with the 1st finger across the 4th, 3rd & 2nd strings. Add your 3rd finger and you have an A6 chord. Then add your 4th finger and an A7 is produced.

Boogie arrangements (like Status Quo's "Rocking All Over The World") often use the normal major chord and add just the 6th note on the 2nd and 4th beats of each bar. Others add the 7th note on the 3rd beat of the bar. These boogie notes can be played on the treble or bass strings as shown in the various chord shapes given:

Heavy Metal Chords

Some of the chords given in this section of the book are what's known as "partial chord shapes" because they come from a common larger shape. Heavy metal rhythm guitarists often use just a few strings and a high volume to produce a strong rhythmic effect and long sustain. Try "cranking up" your guitar and amp and use the partial shapes I've given – when your neighbours are out!

"Layla" by Eric Clapton is a classic song where these kind of heavy metal rhythmic riffs are used – this is notated fully in Book 4 of the "Rock & Pop Guitar" course.

Partial chord shapes are discussed in detail on page 45.

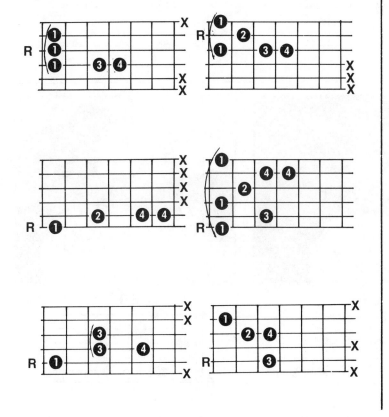

KEY OF A MAJOR
BLUES ROCK / BOOGIE / HEAVY METAL

A7

A7

5th

A9

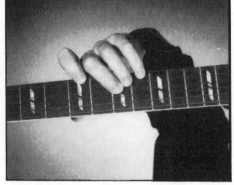
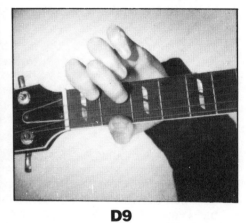

D7

D7

5th

D9

E7

E7

5th

E9

A (add 6/7)

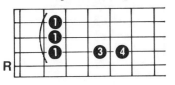

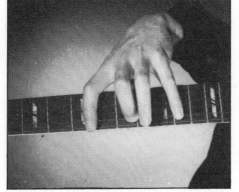

A (add 6/7)

5th

A

5th

A

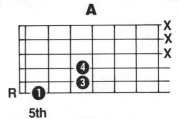

D (add 6/7)

D (add 6/7)

10th

D

5th

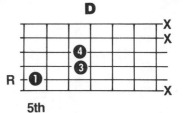

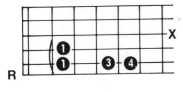

E (add 6/7)

E (add 6/7)

12th

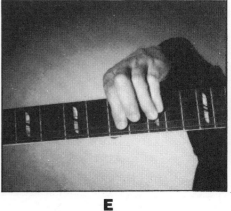

E

7th

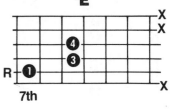

29

KEY OF C MAJOR
BLUES ROCK / BOOGIE / HEAVY METAL

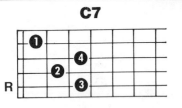
C7

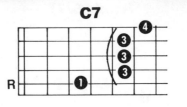
C7

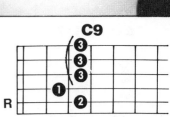
C9

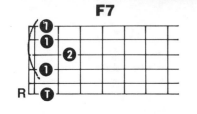
F7

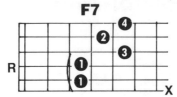
F7

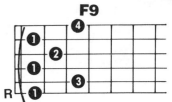
F9

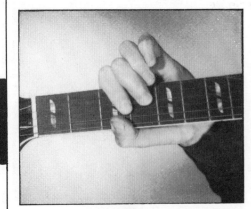

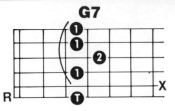
G7

G7

5th

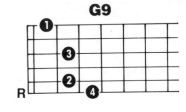
G9

C (add 6)

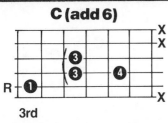

3rd

C (add 6/7)

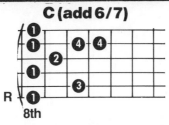

8th

C

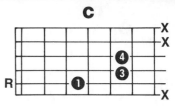

F (add 6)

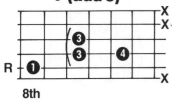

8th

F (add 6/7)

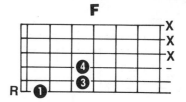

F

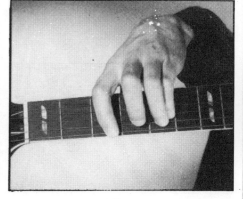

G (add 6)

10th

G (add 6/7)

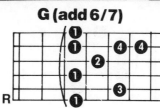

G

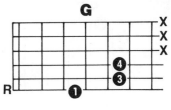

C

F

G

D

D7
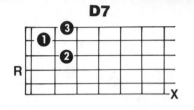

D7
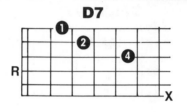

D9
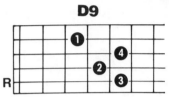

G

G7
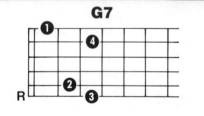

G7
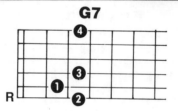

G9

A

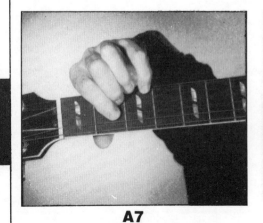

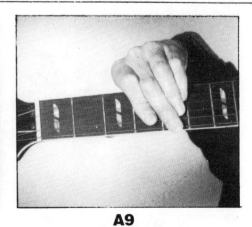

A7
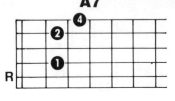

A7
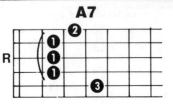

A9
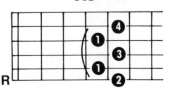

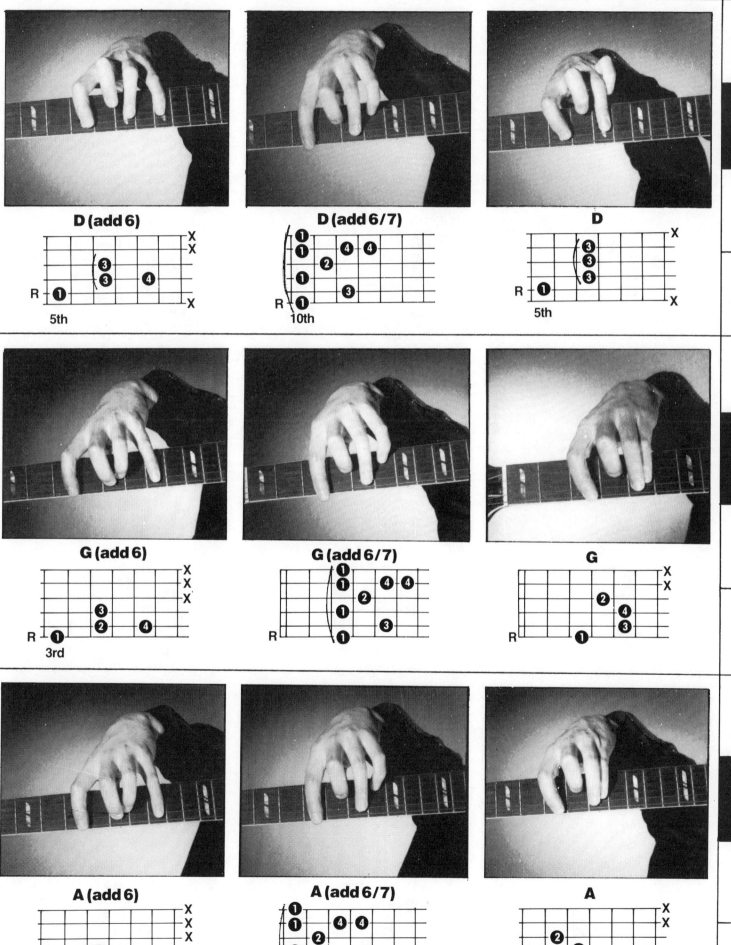

D

G

A

KEY OF F MAJOR
BLUES ROCK / BOOGIE / HEAVY METAL

E

E7

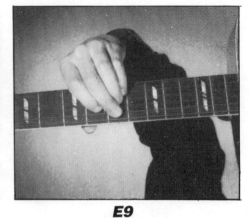

E9

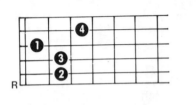

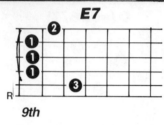

9th

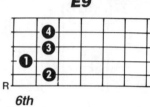

6th

A

A7

A7

A9

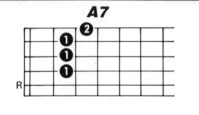

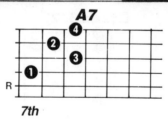

7th

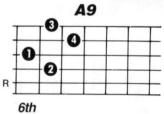

6th

B

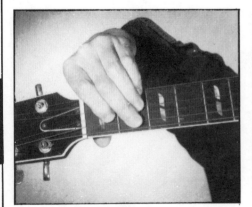

B7

B7

B9

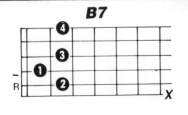

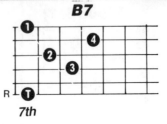

7th

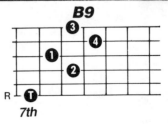

7th

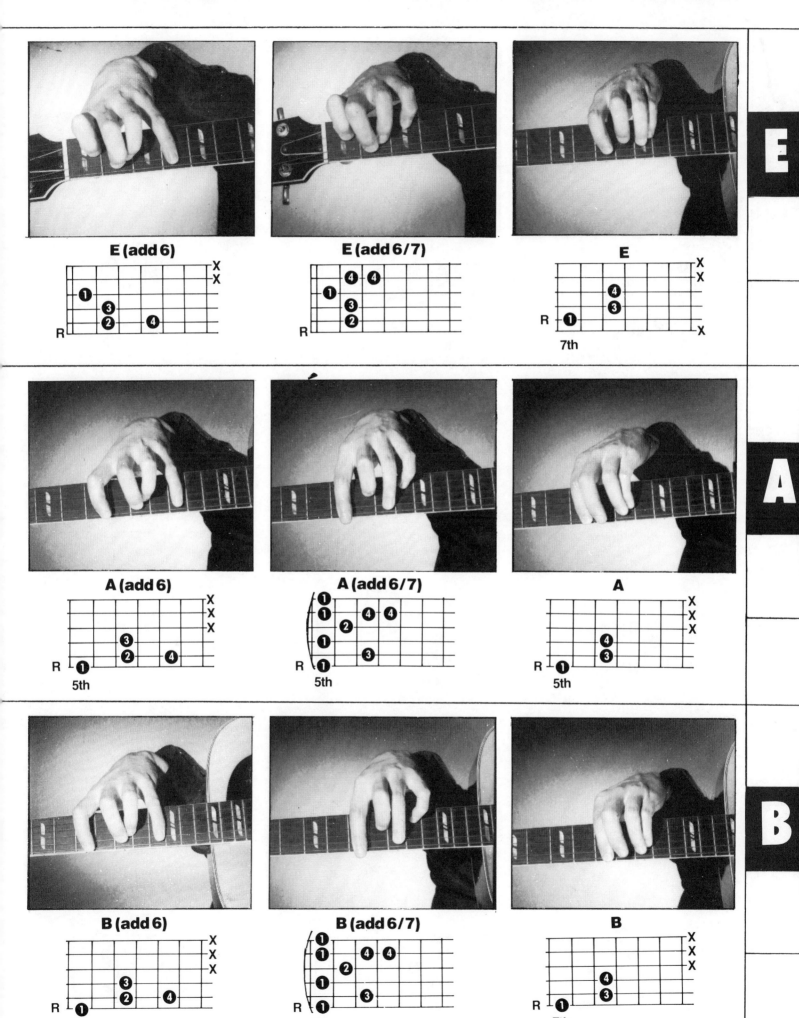

E (add 6)

E (add 6/7)

E

A (add 6)

A (add 6/7)

A

B (add 6)

B (add 6/7)

B

KEY OF G MAJOR
BLUES ROCK / BOOGIE / HEAVY METAL

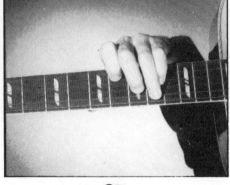

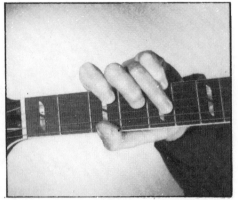

G7   **G7**   **G9**

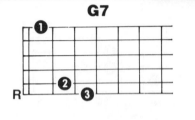
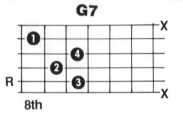
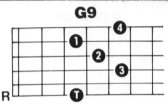

8th

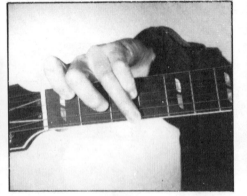

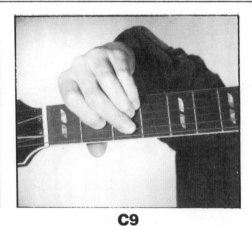

C7   **C7**   **C9**

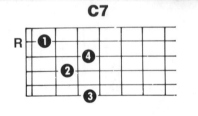
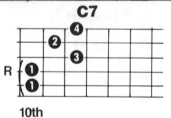

10th

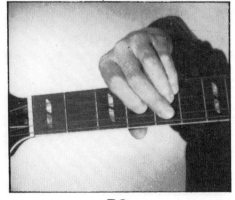

D7   **D7**   **D9**

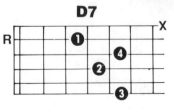
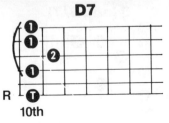
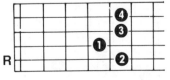

10th

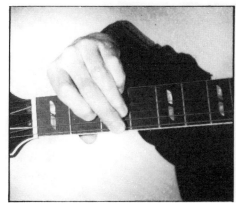

G (add 6/7)

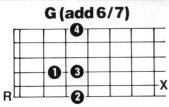

G (add 6/7)

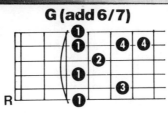

G

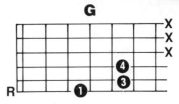

G

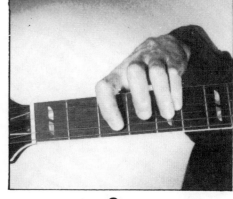

C (add 6/7)

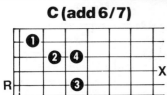

C (add 6/7)

8th

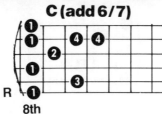

C

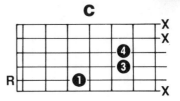

C

D (add 6/7)

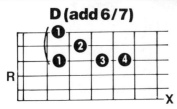

D (add 6/7)

10th

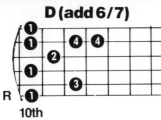

D

5th

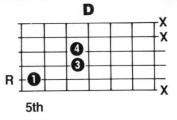

D

MINOR CHORDS
BLUES ROCK / BOOGIE / HEAVY METAL

Am

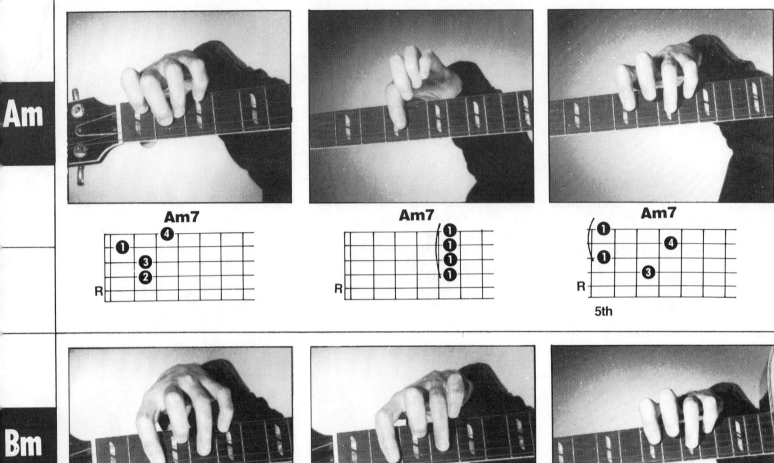

Am7

Am7

Am7

5th

Bm

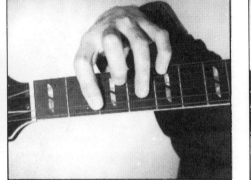

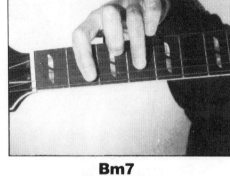

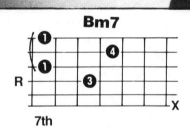

Bm7

Bm7

Bm7

7th

C#m

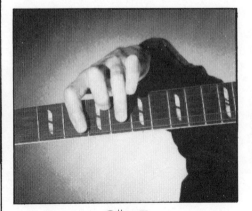

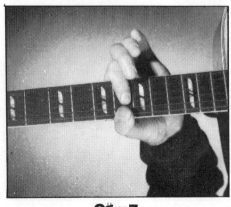

C#m7

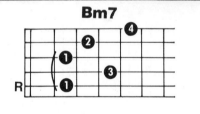

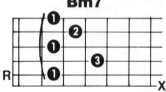

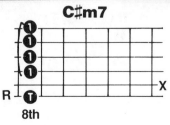

C#m7

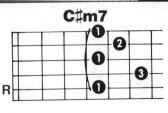

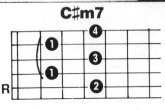

C#m7

8th

MINOR CHORDS
BLUES ROCK / BOOGIE / HEAVY METAL

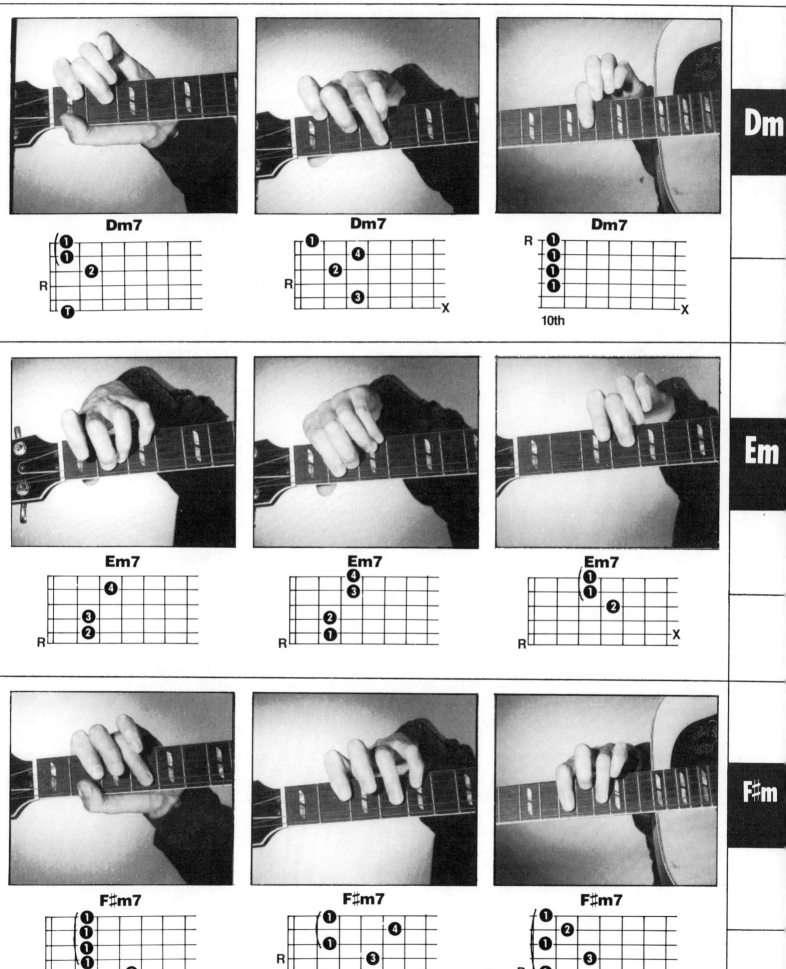

BLUES ROCK / BOOGIE / HEAVY METAL

SAMPLE CHORD SEQUENCE – BOOGIE (Straight Rhythm) 4/4   Band 5, Side 1 on record

Notes: Add the 6th note of each chord on the 2nd & 4th beats of the bar and damp them. Beat marks are given beneath the tablature which is divided into bars. The arrows on the strings represent strums (↑ = downstrum). Use the chord shapes shown above each chord name.

Tablature is explained fully in the introductory book to "Rock & Pop Guitar". The rhythm pattern below and right hand technique is explained in Book 2.

Only 6th notes are added to the chords in this sequence but "blue" notes would be included in lead guitar riffs played over this sequence i.e. the ♭7, ♭3 and ♭5 notes. "d" means the added 6th note must be stopped ringing once sounded i.e. "damped".

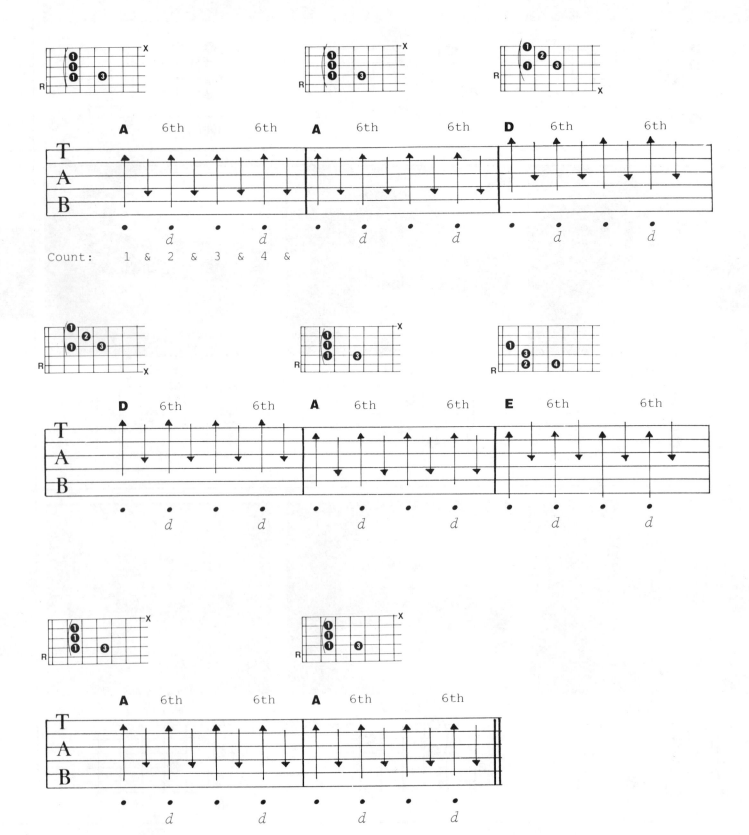

BLUES ROCK / BOOGIE / HEAVY METAL
SAMPLE CHORD SEQUENCE — BLUES SWING 4/4   Band 6, Side 1 on record

Notes: Beat marks are given beneath the tablature which is divided into bars. The numbers on the strings are FRET NUMBERS. Use the chord shapes shown above each chord name.

Tablature is explained fully in the introductory book to "Rock & Pop Guitar". The thumb and fingers style necessary for playing the sequence below is explained in Book 4.

Use the same barred E for the A, A♯ and B chords at the 6th & 7th frets respectively.

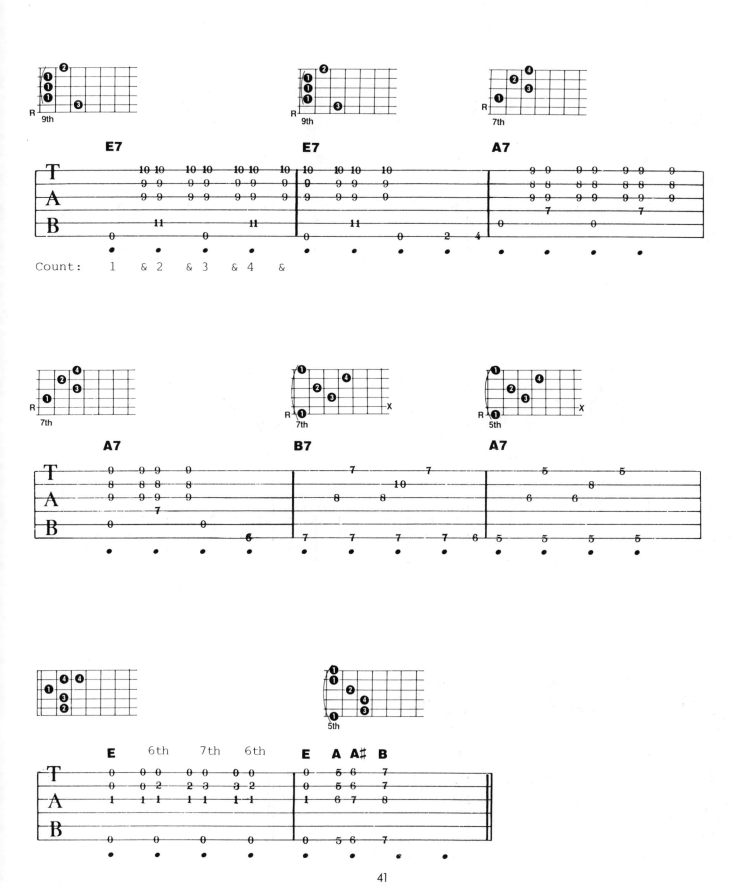

BLUES ROCK/BOOGIE/HEAVY METAL
SAMPLE CHORD SEQUENCE – HEAVY METAL 4/4   Band 7, Side 1 on record

Notes: Chords in heavy metal music are sometimes damped, though not necessarily straight away.

Beat marks are given beneath the tablature which is divided into bars. Arrows on the strings represent strums (↑ = downstrum). Use the chord shapes shown above each chord name.

Tablature is explained fully in the introductory book to "Rock & Pop Guitar". The kind of rhythm and technique below is explained in Book 3.

Ordinary chords (partial shapes) are used in the sequence below, but "blue" notes would be included in lead guitar riffs played over this sequence.

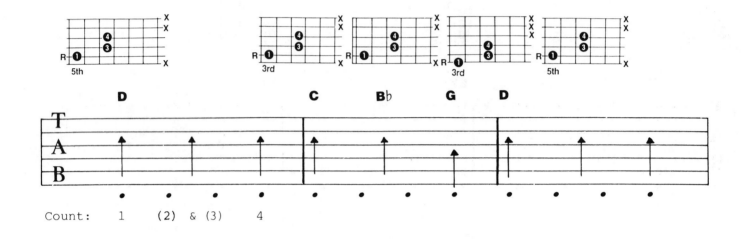

Count: 1   (2) & (3)   4

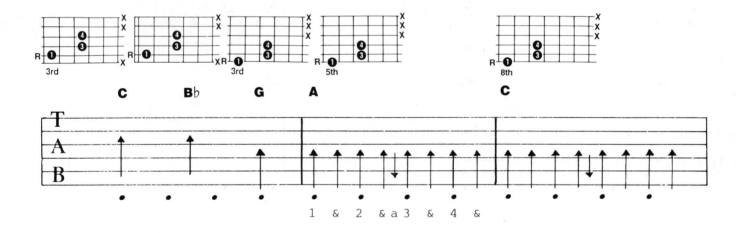

1 & 2 &a 3 & 4 &

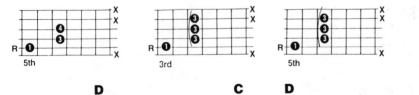

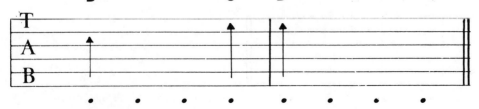

42

CHORD GROUP ③

GENERAL POP / REGGAE / DISCO

GENERAL POP/REGGAE/DISCO

THE MOVEABLE CHORD SHAPE

A

5th

Moveable Shapes

The chords given in this third section of the "Rock & Pop Guitar Chordbook" are what can be called "moveable chord shapes". The most obvious moveable chord shape is one that includes notes on *all* the guitar strings. To be able to handle a variety of general rock and pop accompaniments, you need to know at least these 6-strings moveable shapes:

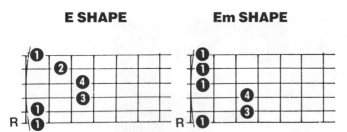

E SHAPE   **Em SHAPE**

The E shape and the equivalent Em shape have their root note on the 6th string. If you can remember or work out the notes on the 6th string you'll be able to use these shapes up and down the fretboard. The E shape shown above at the 5th fret is an A, with its root note A at the 5th fret of the 6th string. See my notes on page 9 if you don't know the guitar fretboard.

The other two main moveable chord shapes you must know have their root on the 5th string:

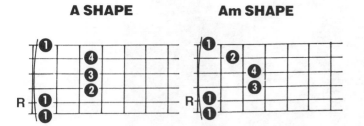

A SHAPE   **Am SHAPE**

The A shape moveable chord has its root on the 5th string, like the easy low position A chord it comes from. The Am shape also has its root note on the 5th string. Thus a Dm chord using the Am shape above is found with a bar at the 5th fret. Similarly, a G chord using the A shape is found with a bar at the 10th fret. NOTICE THAT A MAJOR CHORD SHAPE ALWAYS REMAINS A MAJOR CHORD WHEREVER ON THE FRETBOARD IT IS FINGERED. Likewise, a minor shape remains minor because the relationship of the notes remains the same when the shape remains the same.

Other useful moveable shapes are shown below. You'll notice them occur in the chords given in the 5 keys most used by guitarists. Try to remember the shapes and where their root notes are found.

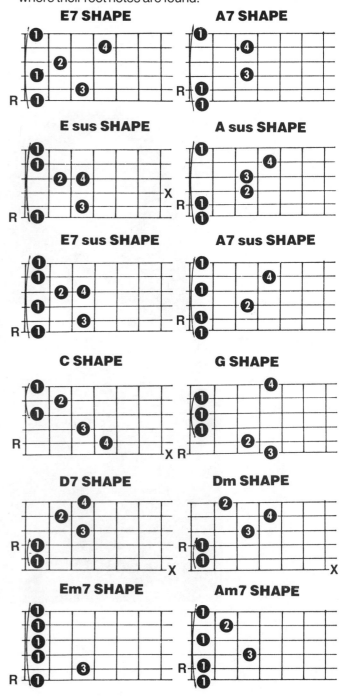

E7 SHAPE   **A7 SHAPE**

E sus SHAPE   **A sus SHAPE**

E7 sus SHAPE   **A7 sus SHAPE**

C SHAPE   **G SHAPE**

D7 SHAPE   **Dm SHAPE**

Em7 SHAPE   **Am7 SHAPE**

GENERAL POP/REGGAE/DISCO

THE PARTIAL CHORD SHAPE

A

5th

Partial Shapes

For reggae and disco rhythm guitar accompaniments partial chord shapes are often used high up the fretboard on the treble strings. A few of these smaller shapes are included in the chords in this section, like the one shown above.

To get a clear, trebly and sharp sound on the guitar it may sometimes be easier and more accurate to use just part of the fuller shapes given in this section. Using smaller shapes also greatly aids speed around the fretboard and leaves one or two fingers free to add notes to chords for variety.

Breaking Up A Full Chord Shape

Each of the 6 or 5 string "full" shapes that you know can be broken up and used in smaller sections. Here is the E shape, for example:

Now here are some partial shapes that are often used in disco, reggae and maybe funk arrangements:

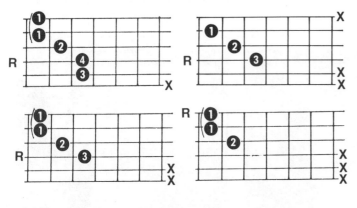

And here are two partial shapes on the bass strings that may be used for rock or heavy metal arrangements (as mentioned in Section 2 of the book):

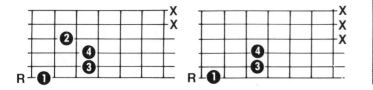

Now try the same idea with a 5 string chord shape:

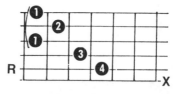

Here are two possiblilites for smaller partial shapes:

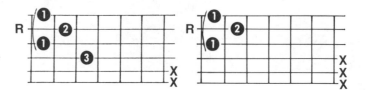

Because there's a spare finger available with partial shapes, a high note can be added – like this, for example:

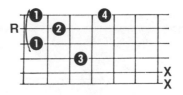

KEY OF A MAJOR
GENERAL POP / REGGAE / DISCO

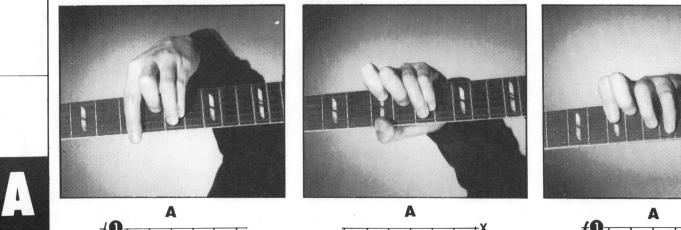

A

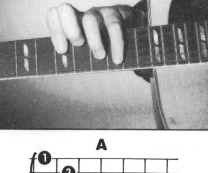

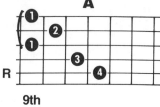

A

1
1
2
4
R   1   3
5th

A

X
1
2
4
R   T   3
5th

A

1
2
1
R   3
     4
9th

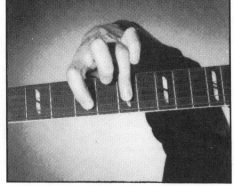

D

1
4
3
2
R   1
     1
5th

D

X
3
3
3
R   1
X
5th

D

1
1
2
4
R   1   3
10th

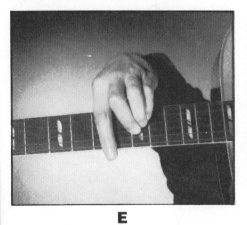

E

1
4
3
2
R   1
     1
7th

E

X
3
3
3
R   1
X
7th

E

1
1
2
R   3
X
12th

46

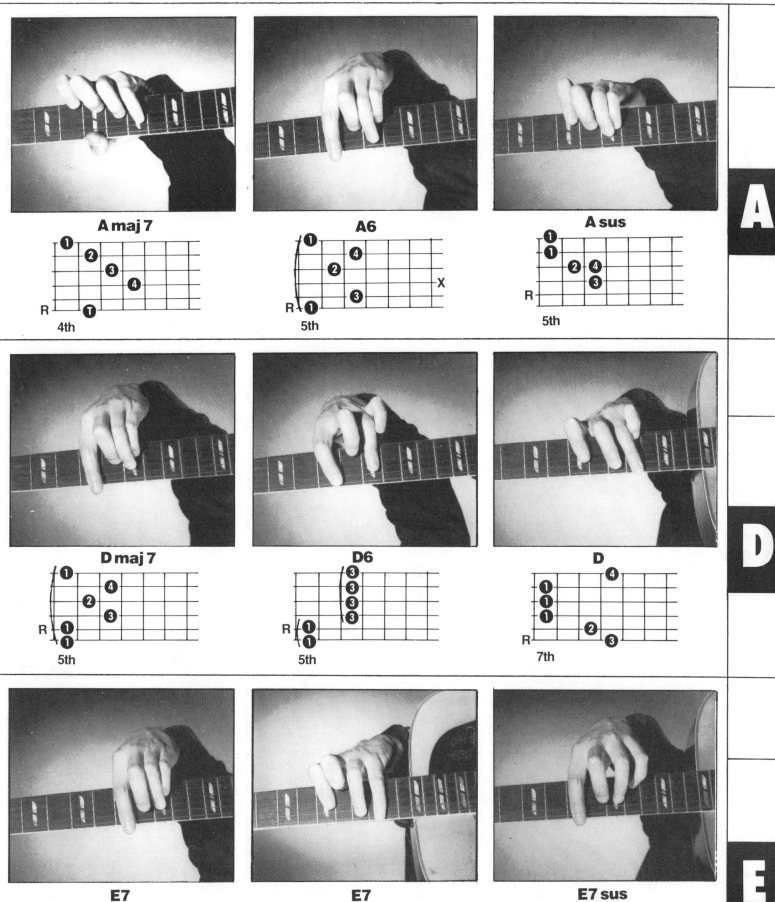

A maj 7 — 4th

A6 — 5th

A sus — 5th

D maj 7 — 5th

D6 — 5th

D — 7th

E7 — 7th

E7 — 9th

E7 sus — 7th

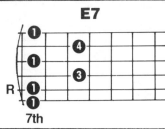

KEY OF C MAJOR
GENERAL POP/REGGAE/DISCO

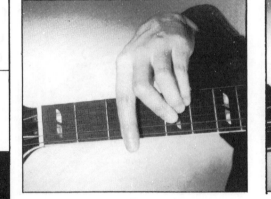

C

C

C

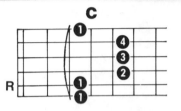

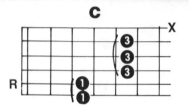

8th

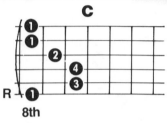

F

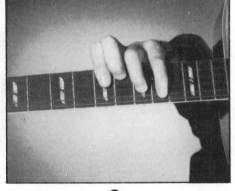

F

F

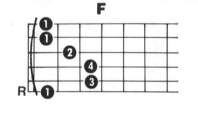

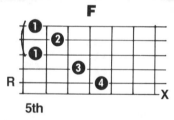

5th

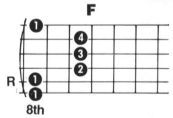

8th

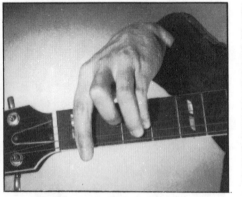

G

G

G

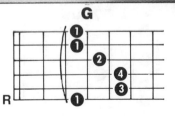

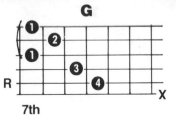

7th

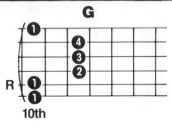

10th

48

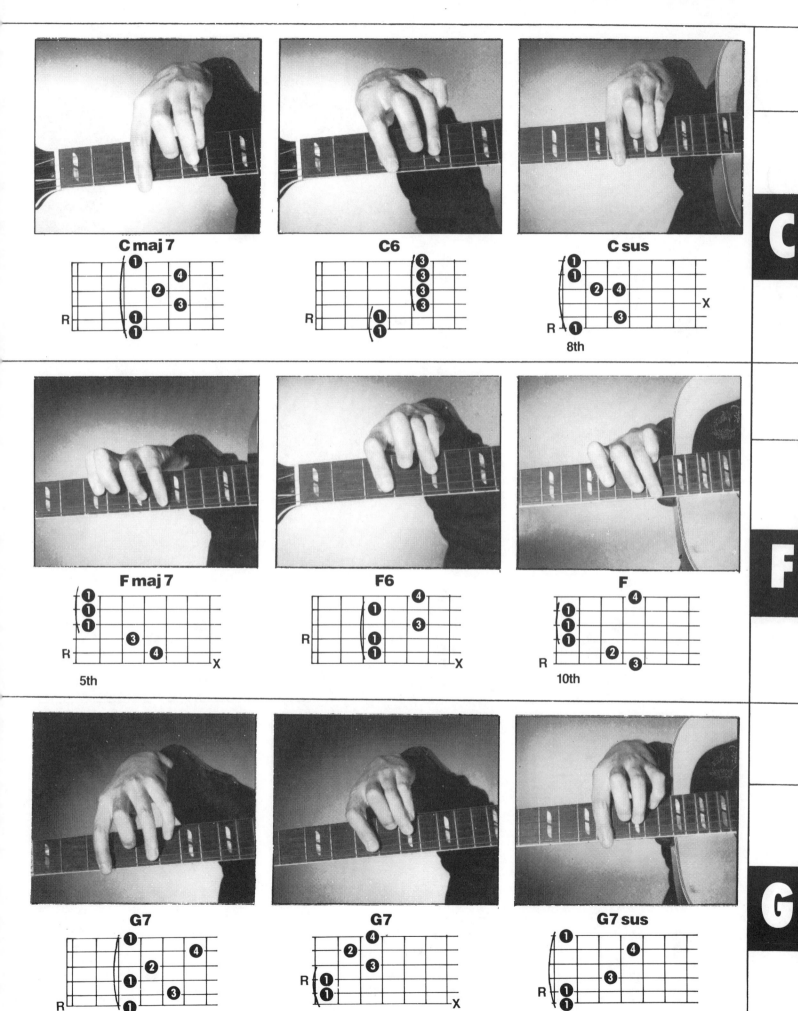

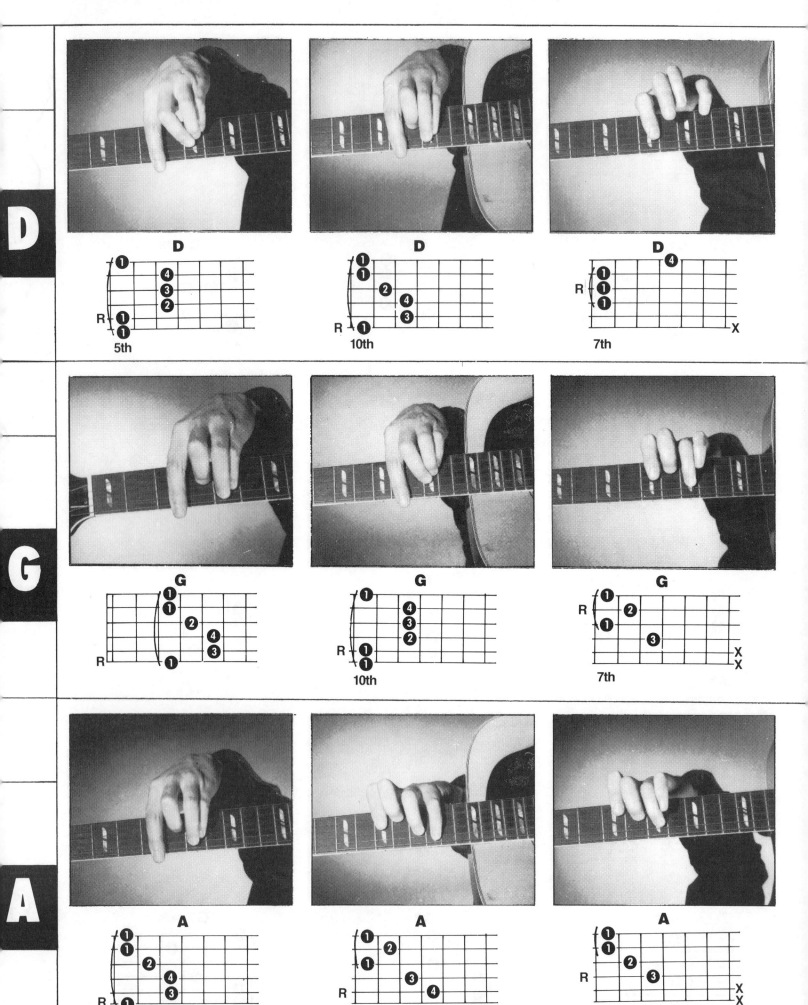

D

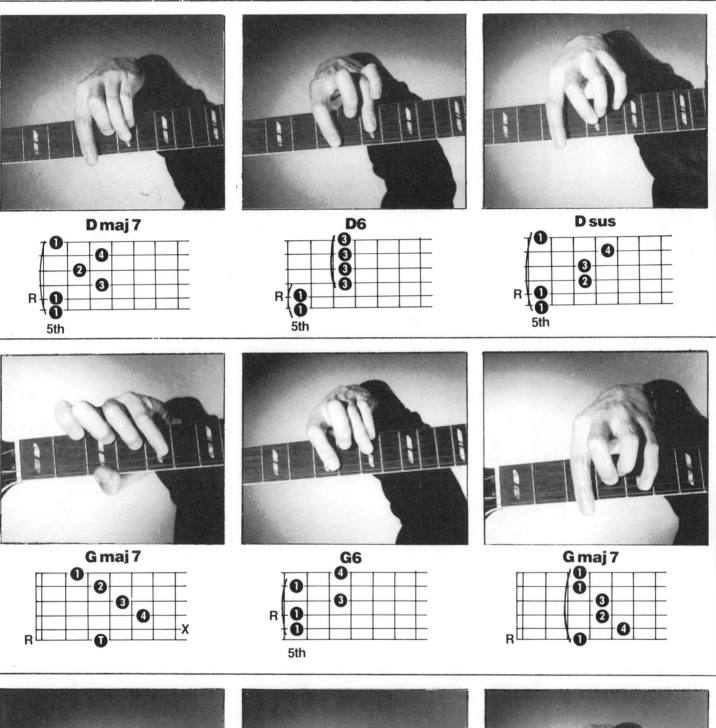

D maj 7

D6

D sus

5th / 5th / 5th

G

G maj 7

G6

G maj 7

5th

A

A7

A7

A7 sus

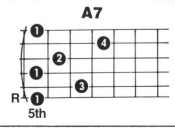

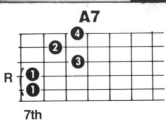

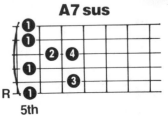

5th / 7th / 5th

KEY OF E MAJOR
GENERAL POP / REGGAE / DISCO

E

 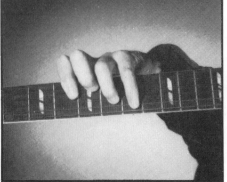 

E — 7th
E — 4th
E — 9th

A

A — 5th
A
A — 9th

B

B — 7th
B
B — 11th

52

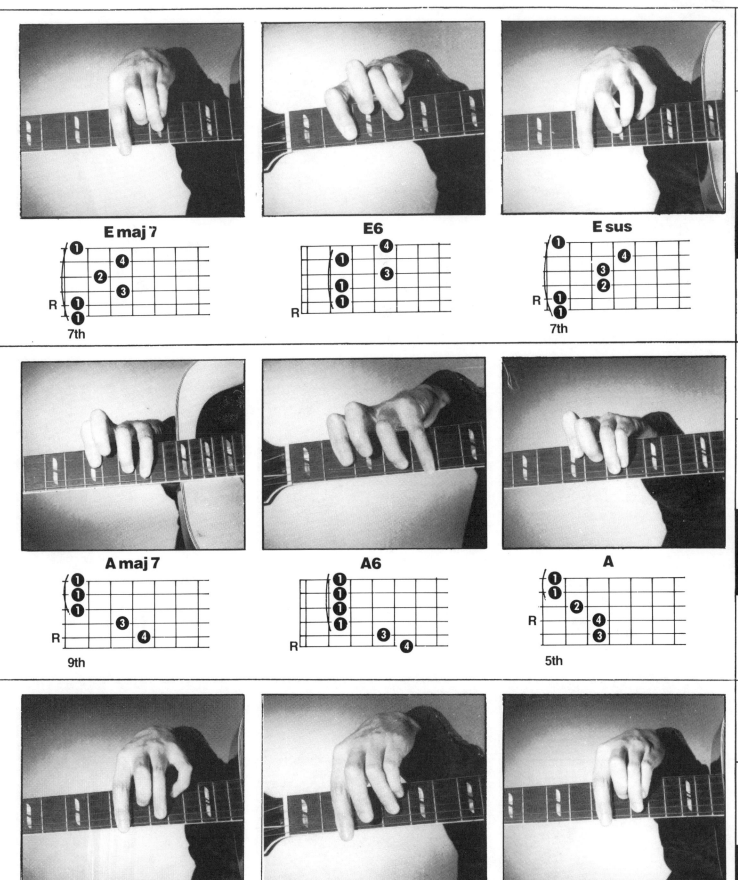

E maj 7

E6

E sus

A maj 7

A6

A

B7

B7

B7 sus

KEY OF G MAJOR
GENERAL POP/REGGAE/DISCO

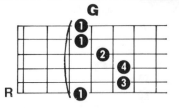

G

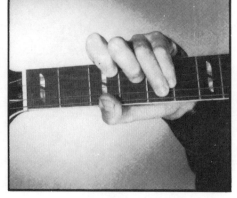

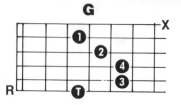

G

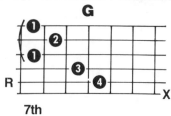

G

7th

C

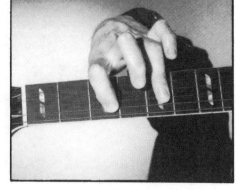

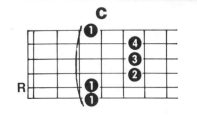

C

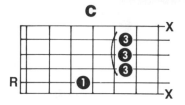

C

8th

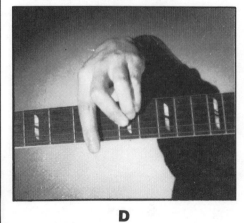

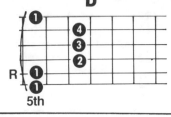

D

5th

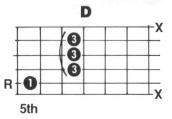

D

5th

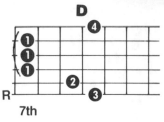

D

7th

GENERAL POP / REGGAE / DISCO

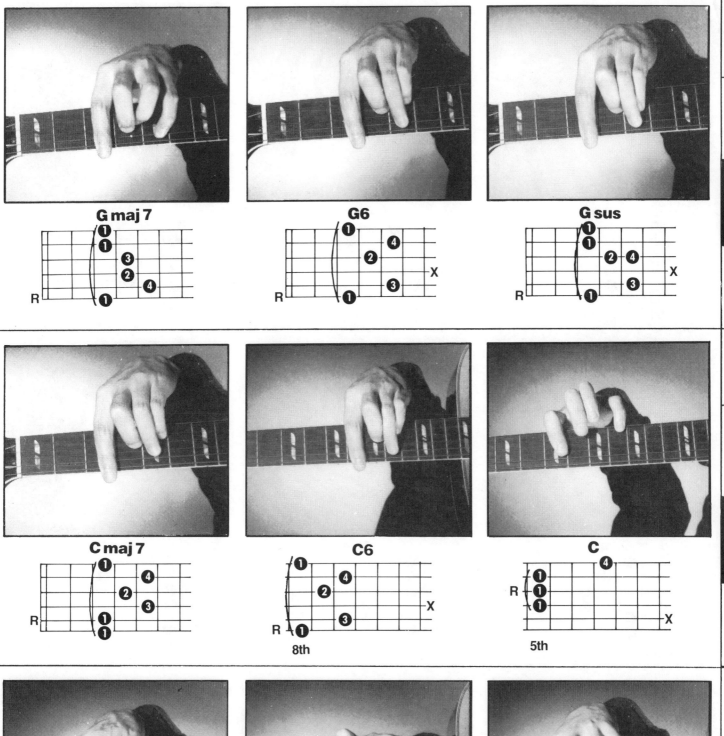

G maj 7

G6

G sus

C maj 7

C6

C

8th

5th

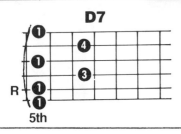

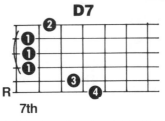

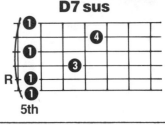

D7

D7

D7 sus

5th

7th

5th

Am

Bm

C#m

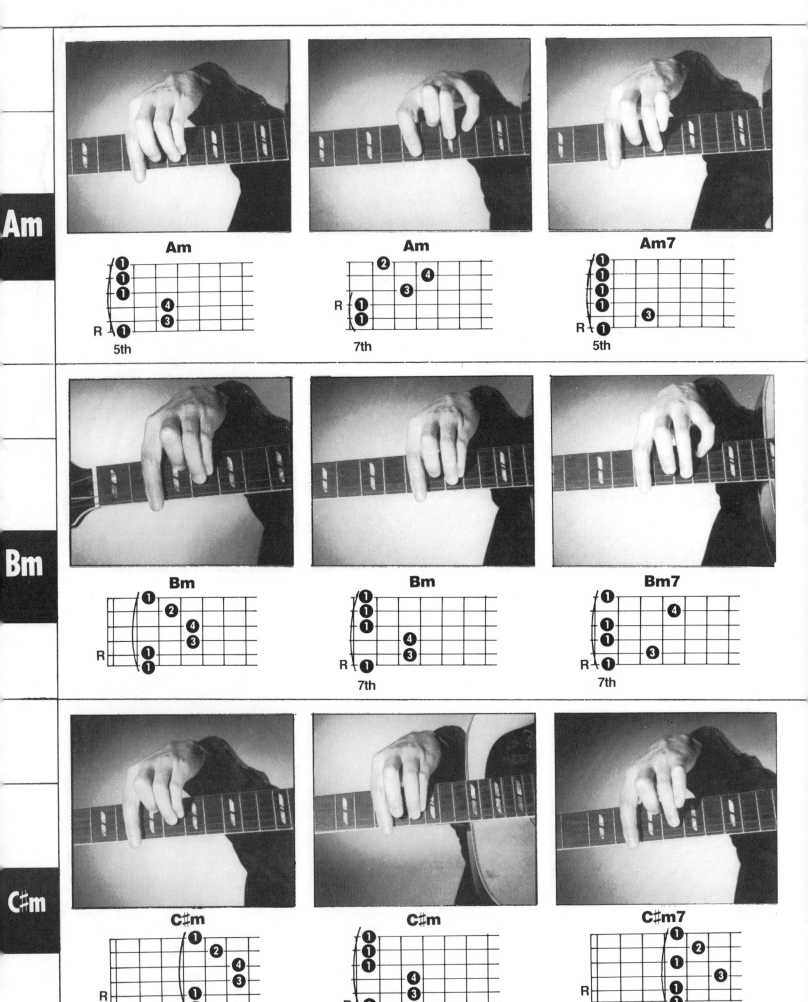

Am — 5th

Am — 7th

Am7 — 5th

Bm

Bm — 7th

Bm7 — 7th

C#m

C#m — 9th

C#m7

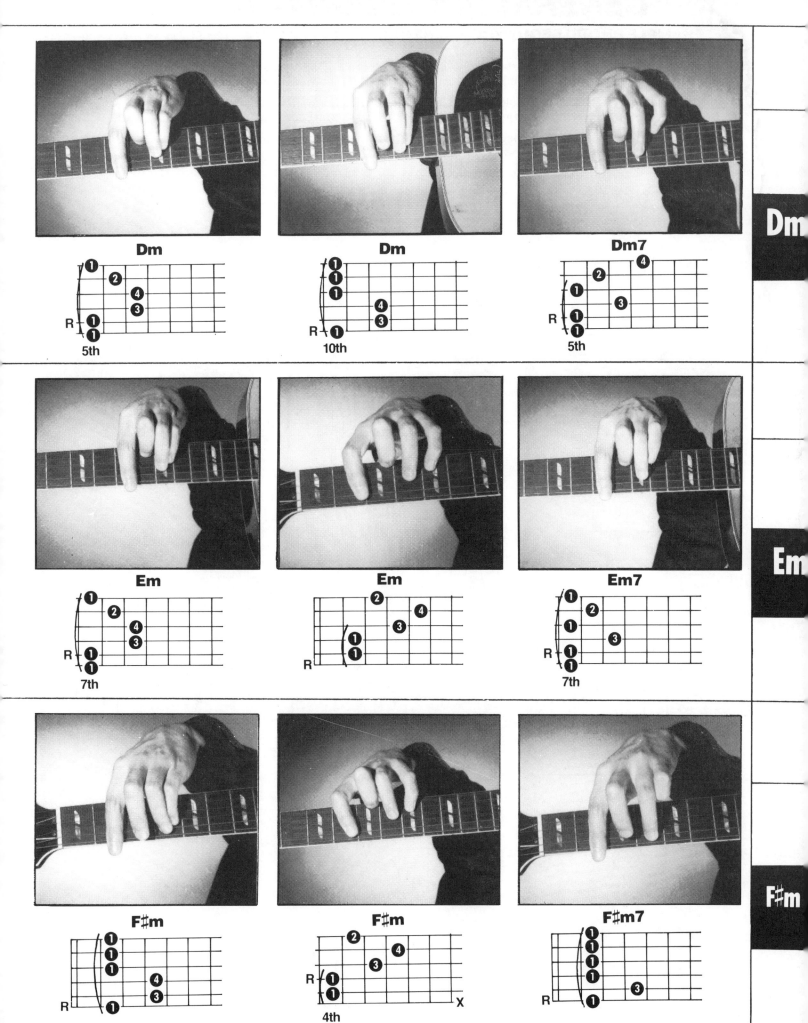

Dm

5th

Dm

10th

Dm7

5th

Em

7th

Em

Em7

7th

F♯m

F♯m

4th

F♯m7

Dm

Em

F♯m

GENERAL POP/REGGAE/DISCO

SAMPLE CHORD SEQUENCE — GENERAL POP BALLAD 4/4   Band 1, Side 2 on record

Notes: Beat marks are given beneath the tablature which is divided into bars. The arrows on the strings represent strums (↑ = downstrum). Use the chord shapes shown above each chord name.

Tablature is explained fully in the introductory book to "Rock & Pop Guitar". The kinds of chord shapes and rhythm patterns used in the sequence below are covered in Books 2 & 3.

When you've mastered this chord sequence using the shapes given, try finding a different set of shapes for the same chords somewhere else on the fretboard.

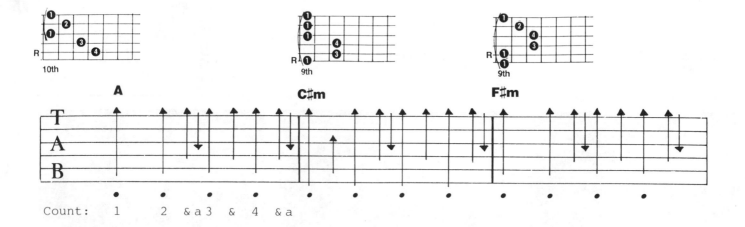

Count: 1   2   & a 3   &   4   & a

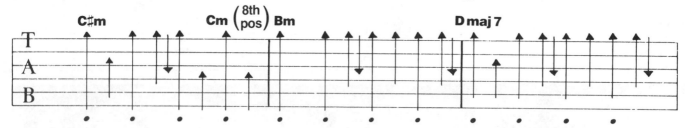

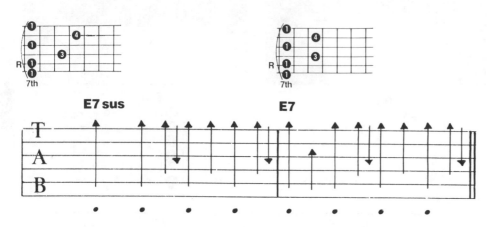

GENERAL POP/REGGAE/DISCO
SAMPLE CHORD SEQUENCE — REGGAE ¢   Band 2, Side 2 on record

Notes: Beat marks are given beneath the tablature which is divided into bars. The arrows on the strings represent strums (↑ = downstrum). Use the chord shapes shown above each chord name.

Tablature is explained fully in the introductory book to "Rock & Pop Guitar". Reggae rhythms and techniques are explained in Book 2.

In reggae guitar the damping technique is often used for the off-beat chops (strums). Damping involves producing a clear sound from the strings and then stopping the notes by releasing the finger pressure on the strings. "d" beneath the strum arrow means a damped strum is needed.

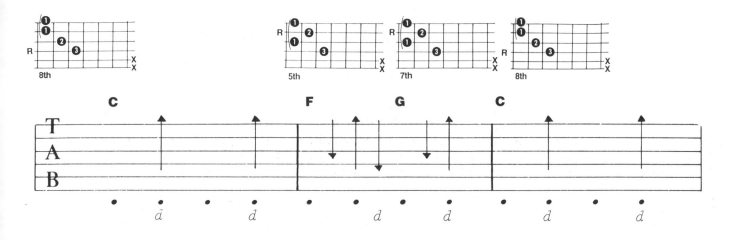

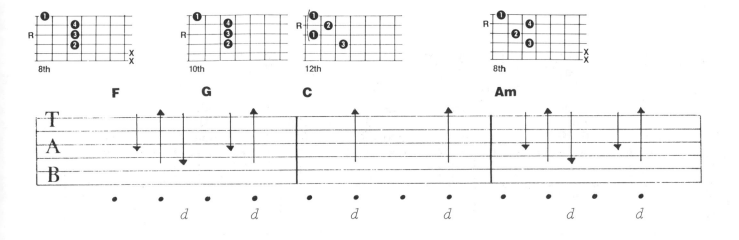

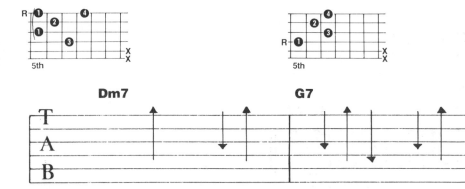

59

GENERAL POP/REGGAE/DISCO

SAMPLE CHORD SEQUENCE—DISCO 4/4   Band 3, Side 2 on record

Notes: Beat marks are given beneath the tablature which is divided into bars. The arrows on the strings represent strums (↑ = downstrum). Use the chord shapes shown above each chord name.

Tablature is explained fully in the introductory book to "Rock & Pop Guitar". The rhythms and techniques of playing disco style guitar are explained in Book 3.

Where a fret position is shown above a chord name (i.e. above F in the 2nd bar), the chord shape used for the chord before should be used again in the fret position given.

The wavy arrows mean muffled strums – the pressure of the fingers on the strings is released but the strings still held.

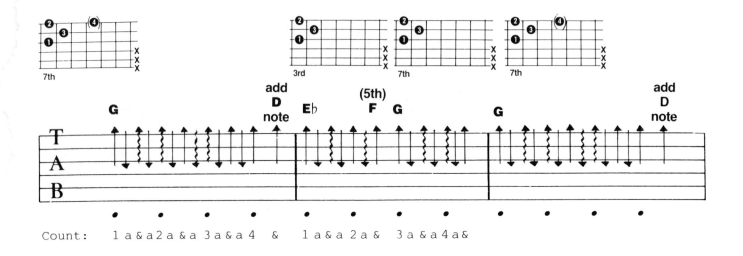

Count: 1 a & a 2 a & a 3 a & a 4 &   1 a & a 2 a &   3 a & a 4 a &

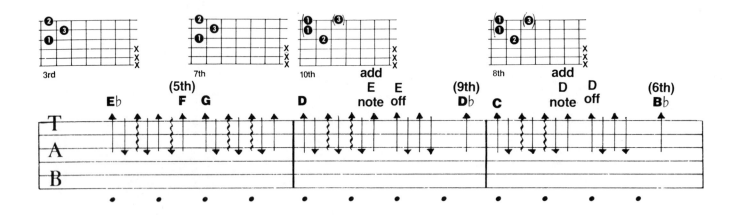

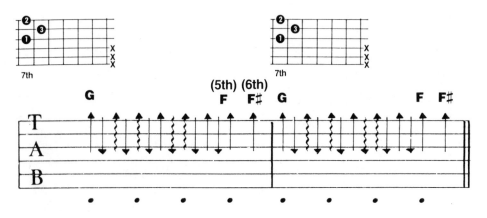

60

CHORD GROUP ④

JAZZ ROCK / LATIN / FUNK

JAZZ ROCK / LATIN / FUNK

CHORD COMPOSITION

A maj 7

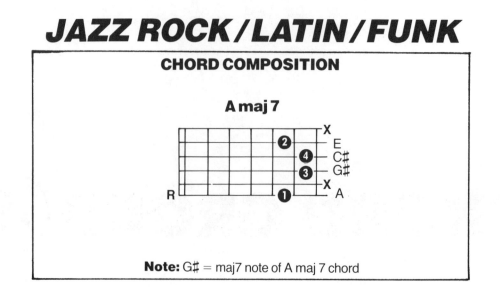

Note: G♯ = maj7 note of A maj 7 chord

The A Maj 7 Chord

The music areas included in this last section of "The Rock & Pop Guitar Chordbook" involve frequent use of extended chords. Perhaps the most popular of these extended chords is the maj7. The Amaj7 chord is shown above. The three basic notes of the A chord are A, C & E – the "1st, 3rd & 5th" in musical parlance because of their position in the A major scale. To these notes is added the major 7th note, in this case G♯, which is the 7th note of the A major scale.

The A6 Chord

The A major 6th (A6 for short), like the Amaj7, is often used as a substitute for the normal A chord – as a I chord of a key or as a IV chord of a key. In other words when A is the key or when A is the IV chord in the key of E.

The A6 chord, like the A maj7, has four notes. The three notes of the A chord, plus the 6th note of the A scale i.e. F♯. Some shapes for the maj6 chords don't have the 5th note, however.

Using the maj7 and maj6 chords as substitutes for the ordinary major chord helps to create interest and movement as well as a more diffuse, jazzy feel. Some major 7th and 6th chord shapes given in this section are often used together – practise changing from one to the other and back again:

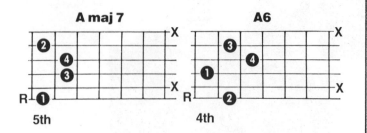

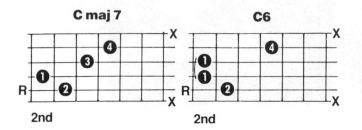

Leave your little finger on when changing from the A maj7 to the A6. For the change from the C maj7 to C6 just remove your 3rd finger and drop down to a bar with your 1st. Many extended chords that are related will have common notes, so always look out for an ANCHOR FINGER.

Inversions

I mentioned inversions on page 8. Where a chord shape is played with the lowest note other than the root or name note of the chord, then it's an inversion. The shapes in this section include a widely used inversion for an ordinary major chord to produce a more diffuse and jazzy flavour. This shape may often be followed by the major 7th shape very similar to it:

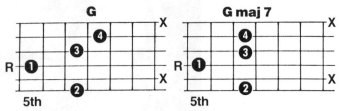

Extended Minor Chords

The music areas covered by this section very often involve the use of extended minor chords. One minor 7th shape is particularly popular, as is the dominant 9th shape that is similar to it:

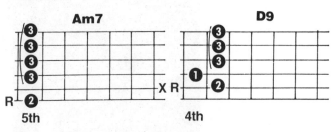

Both these shapes are often slid from a fret below as part of a funk accompaniment, and the D9 often follows the Am7 in a chord sequence. Another common "trick" to add interest and movement is to put on and take off the 9th note (for a minor 9th chord) when holding a minor 7th shape:

m7 (9)

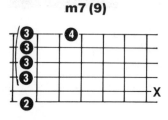

JAZZ ROCK / LATIN / FUNK

MUTING OPEN STRINGS

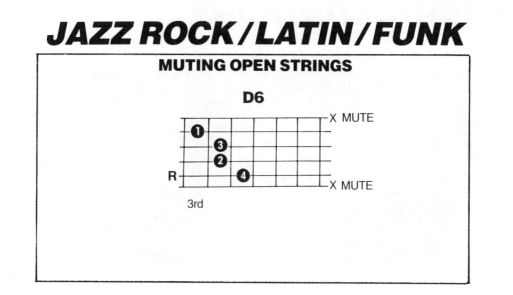

D6

X MUTE

X MUTE

3rd

Muting Strings

When smaller chord shapes are used in certain keys the open string notes may not be part of the chord. In these cases they must not be allowed to sound. For some areas of music (i.e. those covered by Section 1 of this book) the open strings may be allowed to ring as long as they are notes of the chord being played. Thus the E7 chord below can include the open 1st & 6th string E notes:

E7

OPEN

OPEN

R

But when the style of music dictates that open strings shouldn't ring on (see the comments on "damping" later on this page), they must be muted somehow whether or not the notes would be compatible with the chord. Where the 5th or 4th string need to be muted and there's a finger fretting the 6th or 5th string respectively, that finger can drop down slightly to touch the open string and prevent it ringing. As in these popular shapes, for example:

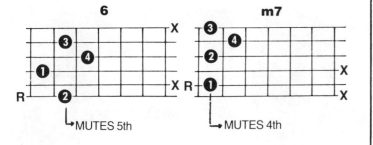

6   **m7**

MUTES 5th   MUTES 4th

When strumming across the strings for a smooth and continuous flowing rhythm, you need to be able to strum right across all the strings and not be inhibited by the possibility of sounding open string notes that would clash with the chord. Thus open top and bottom strings, as in the E7 chord already mentioned, must also be muted. The open 6th string can always be muted by the thumb, which is brought over from the back of the neck till the pad of the top joint touches the 6th string and stops it from sounding.– see the photo for the maj 6th chord above.

The open 1st string can be damped in various slightly different ways. Where the 1st finger is fretting the 2nd string, it can be brought down a little flatter so the pad of the top joint touches and mutes the 1st string – like a finger mutes one of the middle 4 strings.

Where the 1st finger is fretting a string other than the 2nd, the lower joint of the 1st or 2nd finger can be brought closer to the guitar neck so it touches the 1st string. Try that for these shapes:

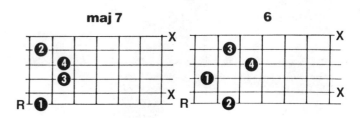

maj 7   **6**

Where there's a half bar, the first (or other barring finger) can be brought down to touch the 1st string hard enough to deaden it but not produce a clear note:

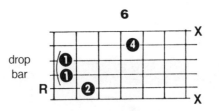

6

drop
bar

R

Damping

Damping is not the same as muting – damping is guitarists' jargon for stopping notes *after* clear sounds have been produced. For many modern strumming guitar styles damping is absolutely essential to produce the required effects. Rhythmic effects like syncopation and stress dynamics are made powerful with the damping technique. Try strumming across some of the shapes given in this section, with the left hand fingers down firmly till just after the strum and clear notes have been produced. Then release the left hand finger pressure on the strings, but don't let go of them. Music theorists would call the effect "staccato". While damping the strings don't forget also to mute those open strings you don't want to sound!

KEY OF A MAJOR
JAZZ ROCK / LATIN / FUNK

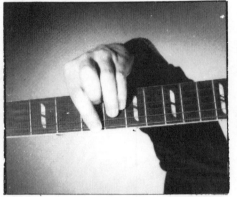

A maj 7

A6

A maj 7

7th

A

D maj 7

4th

D maj 7

D maj 7

10th

D

E7

5th

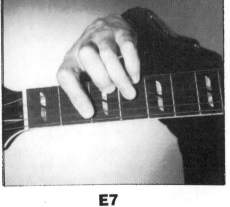

E7

E7

7th

E

64

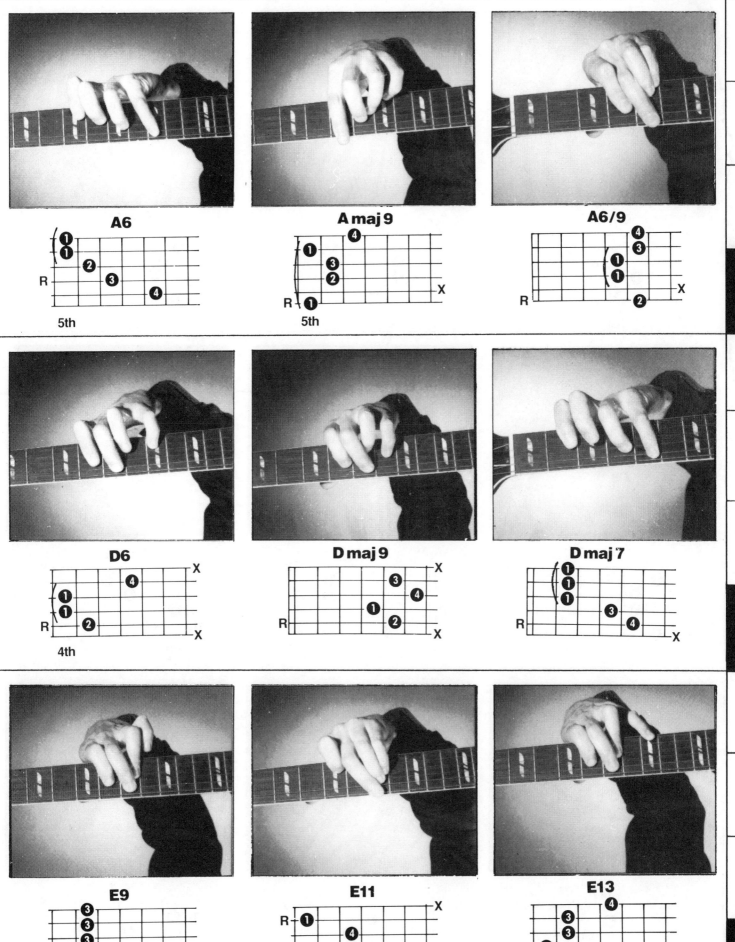

C

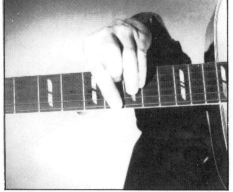

C maj 7

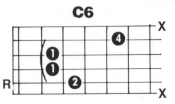

C6

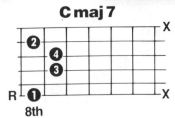

C maj 7

8th

F

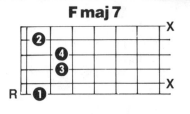

F maj 7

F maj 7

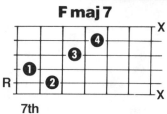

F maj 7

7th

G

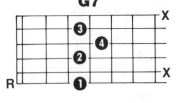

G7

G7

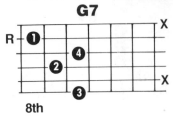

G7

8th

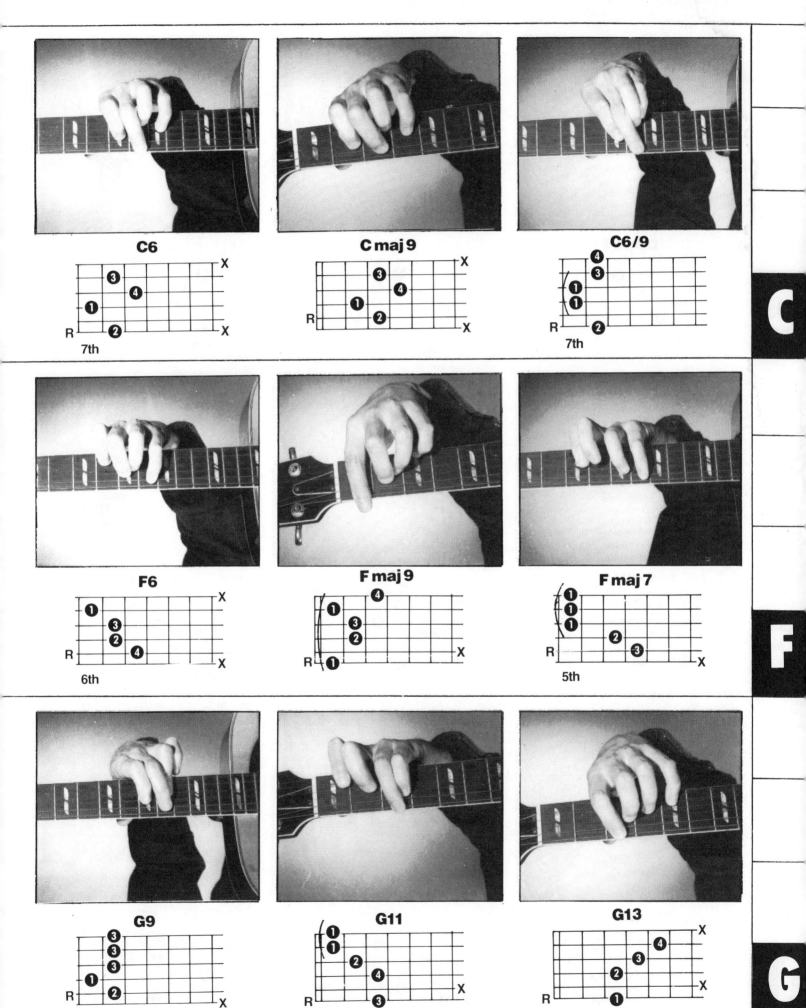

C6

7th

C maj 9

C6/9

7th

F6

6th

F maj 9

F maj 7

5th

G9

9th

G11

G13

C

F

G

KEY OF D MAJOR
JAZZ ROCK / LATIN / FUNK

D

D maj 7

4th

D6

D maj 7

10th

G

G maj 7

G6

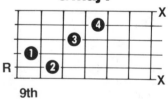

G maj 7

9th

A

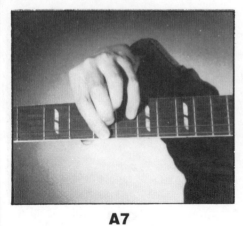

A7

A7

5th

A7

7th

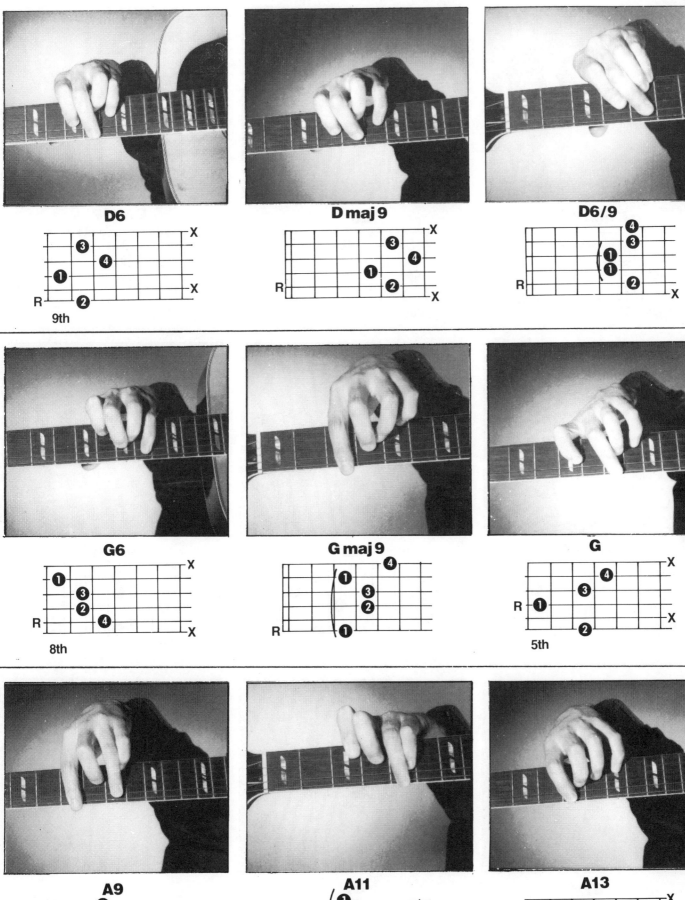

D6

9th

D maj 9

D6/9

G6

8th

G maj 9

G

5th

A9

5th

A11

A13

5th

D

G

A

KEY OF E MAJOR
JAZZ ROCK / LATIN / FUNK

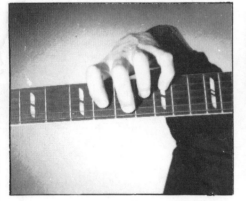

E maj 7

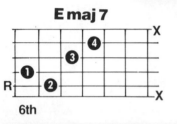

6th

E6

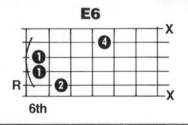

6th

E maj 7

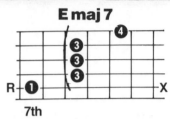

7th

A maj 7

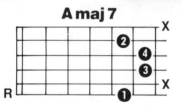

A6

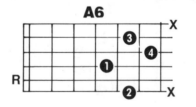

A maj 7

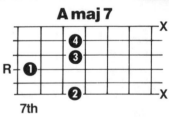

7th

B7

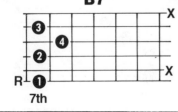

7th

B7

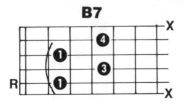

B7

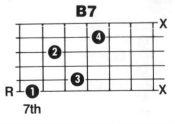

7th

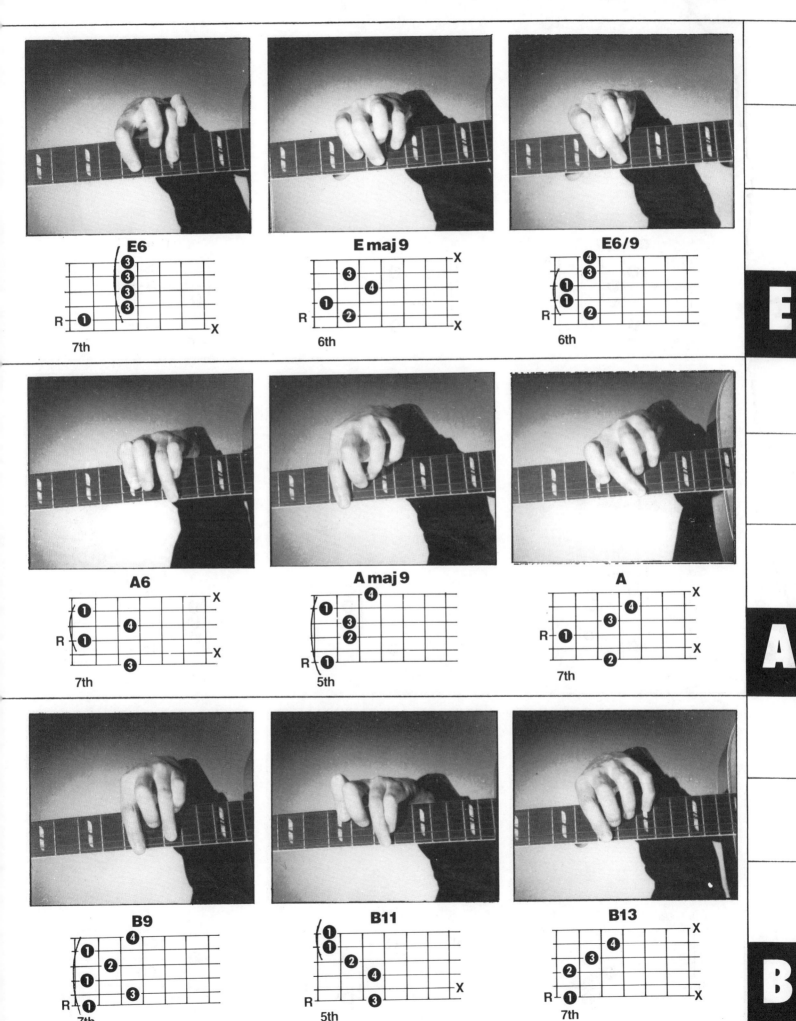

E6

7th

E maj 9

6th

E6/9

6th

A6

7th

A maj 9

5th

A

7th

B9

7th

B11

5th

B13

7th

E

A

B

KEY OF G MAJOR
JAZZ ROCK / LATIN / FUNK

G

G maj 7

G6

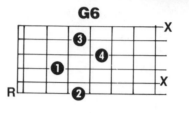

G maj 7

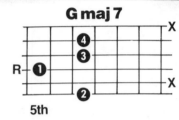

5th

C

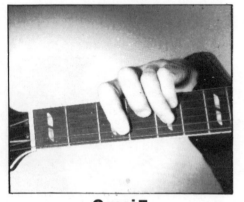

C maj 7

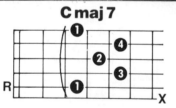

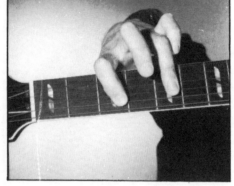

C6

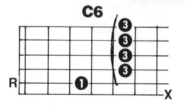

C maj 7

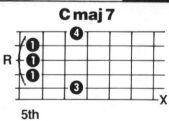

5th

D

D7

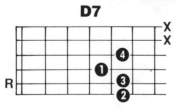

D7

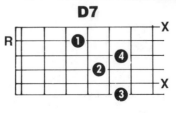

D7

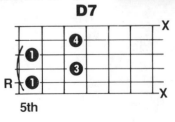

5th

72

G6

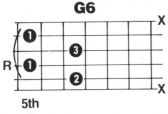

5th

G maj 9

G6/9

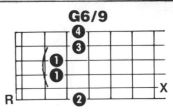

G

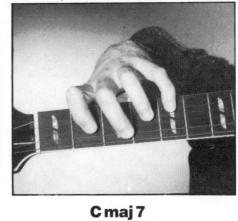

C6

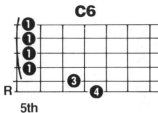

5th

C maj 9

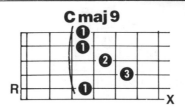

C maj 7

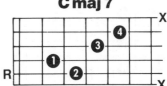

C

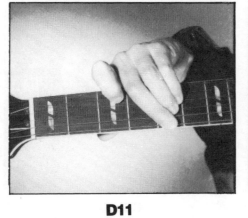

D9

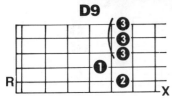

D11

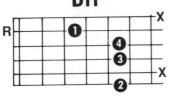

D13

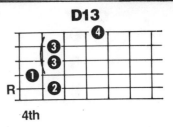

4th

D

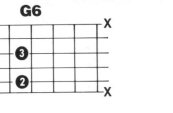

MINOR CHORDS
JAZZ ROCK / LATIN / FUNK

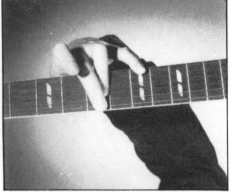

Am7
Am6
Am9

5th

Bm7
Bm6
Bm9

7th

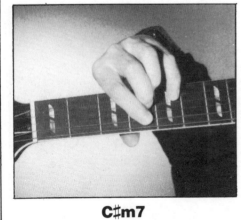

C#m7
C#m6
C#m9

Am

Bm

C#m

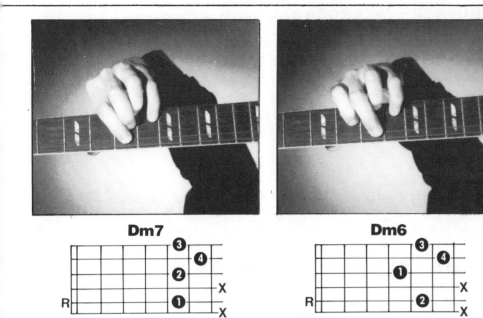

Dm7

Dm6

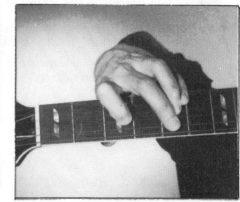

Dm9

Dm

Em7

7th

Em6

6th

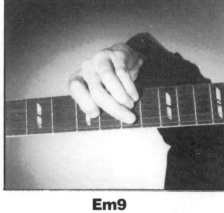

Em9

5th

Em

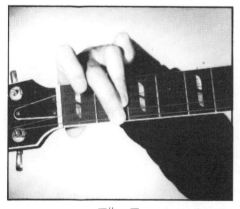

F♯m7

F♯m6

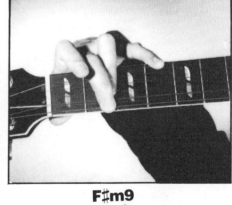

F♯m9

F♯m

JAZZ ROCK / LATIN / FUNK

SAMPLE CHORD SEQUENCE — JAZZ ROCK 4/4 Band 4, Side 2 on record

Notes: Beat marks are given beneath the tablature which is divided into bars. The arrows on the strings represent strums (↑ = downstrum). Use the chord shapes shown above each chord name.

Tablature is explained fully in the introductory book to "Rock & Pop Guitar". The rhythms and techniques of playing jazz rock are covered in Books 3 & 4.

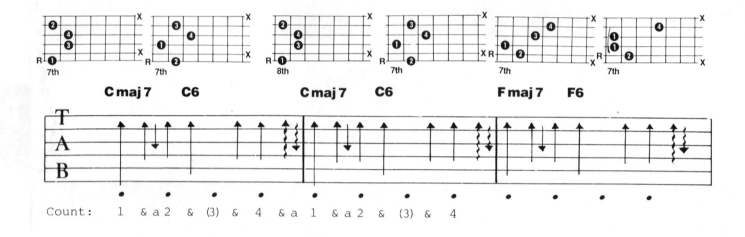

Count: 1 & a 2 & (3) & 4 & a 1 & a 2 & (3) & 4

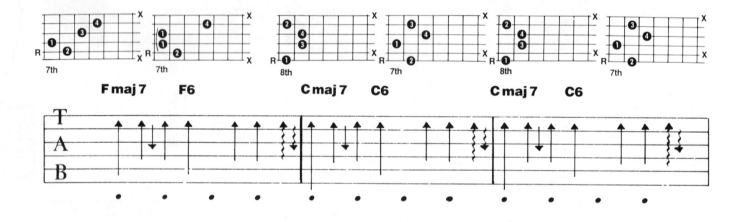

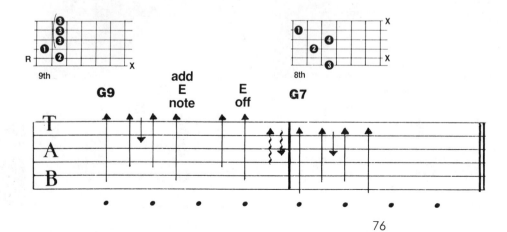

76

JAZZ ROCK / LATIN / FUNK
SAMPLE CHORD SEQUENCE – FUNK 4/4 Band 5, Side 2 on record

Notes: Beat marks are given beneath the tablature which is divided into bars. The arrows on the strings represent strums (↑ = downstrum). The numbers on the strings are FRET NUMBERS. Use the chord shapes shown above each chord name.

"d" means the strings should be sounded then stopped quickly. Tablature is explained fully in the introductory book to "Rock & Pop Guitar".

Funk guitar styles and techniques are covered in Book 3.

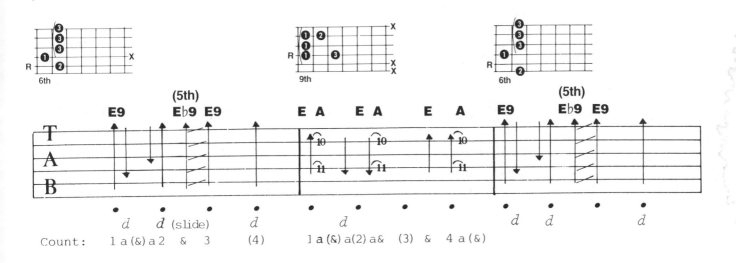

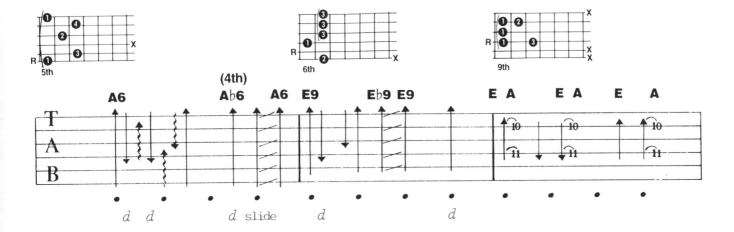

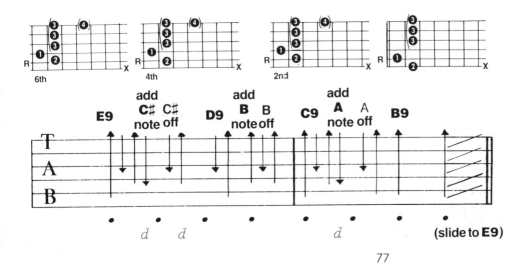

JAZZ ROCK / LATIN / FUNK
SAMPLE CHORD SEQUENCE — LATIN 4/4   Band 6, Side 2 on record

Notes: Beat marks are given beneath the tablature which is divided into bars. The arrows on the strings represent slaps with the right hand. The numbers on the strings are FRET NUMBERS. Use the chord shapes shown above each chord name. Tablature is explained fully in the introductory book to "Rock & Pop Guitar".

The slap style is covered in Book 4.

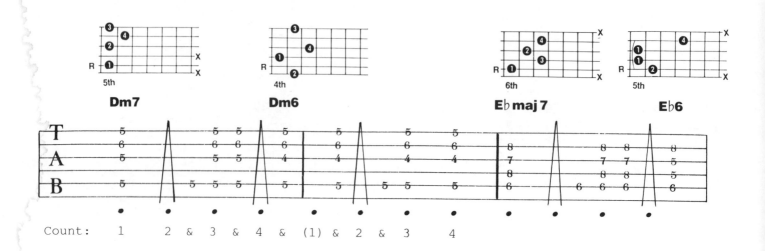

Dm7   Dm6   Eb maj 7   Eb6

Count: 1   2 & 3 & 4 & (1) & 2 & 3   4

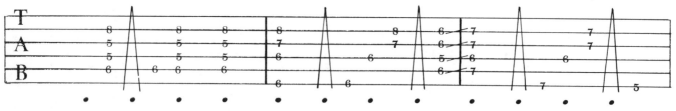

Eb6   Bb13   Eb9 E9   A7

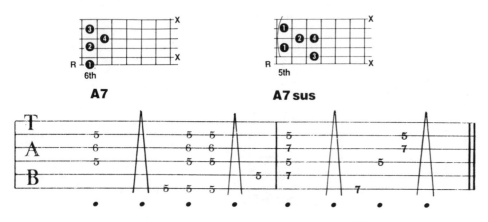

A7   A7 sus

78

OTHER IMPORTANT CHORDS

Diminished 7th Chord Shapes

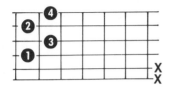 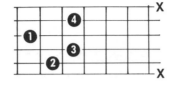 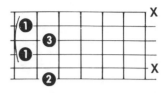

The root note of the diminished chord could be any one of the four shown, depending on context. Because 3 of the 4 notes are common to the dominant 7th chord, it can be used as a substitute for the dominant 7th sometimes. The diminished chord can be used effectively as a passing chord i.e. C to C♯dim7 to Dm.

Augmented Chord Shapes

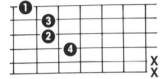

Though the shapes shown above for the augmented chord (known as A+ or A aug for example) include 4 or 5 strings, only three notes are involved. Like the diminished chord, any of the augmented chord notes can be the root, depending on context. Augmented chords can be used effectively as passing chords i.e. in a descending minor chord progression – Em to B+ to Em7, or in a II V I chord sequence like Dm to G+ to C.

M7♭5 Chord Shapes

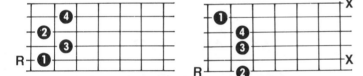

The minor 7th flat 5 chord can be used as a substitute for the dominant 7th chord of the key it's in i.e. Bm7♭5 for G7 in the key of C. It can be used as part of a progression as well, like Em to F♯mb5 to B7 to Em.

Dom 7th ♭5 Chord Shapes

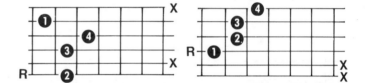

The dominant 7th flat 5 chord may sometimes be used as a substitute for the usual dominant 7th chord i.e. A7b5 instead of A7. It can also be used in chord sequences like Em to A7b5 to Dm.

Transposing Chord Accompaniments

On page 9 I showed you how to change the key of an accompaniment using the capo. It's not too difficult to change key *without* a capo, and it's a very useful skill to have.

If you have one set of chords for a song like A, D & E for example, and you want to go up in pitch just a little, try the equivalent chords in C. Thus you've gone up in pitch by three semitones (or frets) from the key of A to the key of C. The other chords must go up in pitch by 3 semitones too – so D becomes F and E becomes G.

When you're changing the pitch of a song by a reasonable amount, you should count up from the original key to the new one in letters only at first. Changing from A to E could be counted like this:

A	B	C	D	Ⓔ
1	2	3	4	5

This is called a "5th" higher in musical terms. The other chords must go up by the same amount:

D	E	F	G	Ⓐ
1	2	3	4	5
E	F	G	A	Ⓑ

REMEMBER THAT MAJOR CHORDS STAY MAJOR CHORDS, 7TH CHORDS REMAIN 7THS, MINOR CHORDS STAY MINOR and so on.

If the new chord doesn't sound right with the others, check the exact number of semitones or frets between the root notes, or try the chord a fret higher or lower.

Less Used Keys

You may occasionally have to play in a key other than the usual 5 included in this book. Try changing these chords in the key of C to the key of E♭ Major, for example:

	C	Am	Dm	G7	C maj 7
become:	E♭	Cm	Fm	Bb7	Ebmaj7

[C to E♭ = 3 semitones or frets]

Now find the appropriate moveable shape for each chord i.e. the C shape for the E♭, with a bar at the 3rd fret.

CHORD COMPOSITION SUMMARY

MAJOR SCALE OF ROOT NOTE

	t		t		s/t		t		t		t		s/t	
Major Scale Notes	DO		RE		MI		FA		SO		LA		TI	DO
Scale Step	1		$2_{(9)}$		3		$4_{(11)}$		5		$6_{(13)}$		7	$8_{(1)}$
Example – A Major Scale	A		B		C♯		D		E		F♯		G♯	A

Root Note Scale

When analysing a chord, the notes are compared to the major scale of the root. In other words, all the chords that have an A root note are analysed in relation to the notes of an A Major scale – as shown above. To produce a major scale for any note, the intervals shown above must be produced i.e. tone, tone, semitone, tone, tone, tone, semitone. Notes need to be made sharp or flat to create these intervals. One fret on the guitar = one semitone.

Chord Extensions

As shown above, the 2nd, 4th & 6th notes are sometimes known as 9th, 11th & 13th notes – this is when they are added to chords already extended. On the guitar extended chords are often called "9ths", "11ths" or "13ths" even though these added notes may not be over an octave higher than the root. On or more notes may be dropped from 9th, 11th or 13th chords to accommodate them on the guitar. A summary of the chords in this book and their composition is shown below.

GENERAL		EXAMPLE – A ROOT NOTE CHORDS	
CHORD TYPE	**NOTES IN CHORD**	**CHORD NAME**	**NOTES IN CHORD**
MAJOR CHORDS			
MAJOR	– 1 3 5	A	– A C♯ E
MAJOR 6th	– 1 3 5 6	A6	– A C♯ E F♯
MAJOR 7th	– 1 3 5 7	A maj 7	– A C♯ E G♯
MAJOR 9th	– 1 3 5 7 9	A maj 9	– A C♯ E G♯ B
MAJOR 6/9	– 1 3 5 6 9	A6/9	A C♯ E F♯ B
DOMINANT CHORDS			
DOMINANT MAJOR	– 1 3 5	A	– A C♯ E
DOMINANT 7th	– 1 3 5 ♭7	A7	– A C♯ E G
DOMINANT 9th	– 1 3 5 ♭7 9	A9	– A C♯ E G B
DOMINANT 11th	– 1 3 5 ♭7 9 11	A11	– A C♯ E G B D
DOMINANT 13th	– 1 3 5 ♭7 9 11 13	A13	– A C♯ E G B D F♯
MINOR CHORDS			
MINOR	– 1 ♭3 5	Am	– A C E
MINOR 6th	– 1 ♭3 5 6	Am6	– A C E F♯
MINOR 7th	– 1 ♭3 5 ♭7	Am7	– A C E G
MINOR 9th	– 1 ♭3 5 ♭7 9	Am9	– A C E G B
OTHER CHORDS			
DIMINISHED 7th	– 1 ♭3 ♭5 ♭♭7	A dim	– A C E♭ G♭♭ (F)
AUGMENTED	– 1 3 ♯5	A aug	– A C♯ E♯ (F)
SUSTAINED 4th	– 1 4 5	A sus	– A D E

Printed by Watkiss Studios Ltd., Biggleswade, Beds. 1/90